LEARNER'S PSYCHOLOGY

FOUNDATION OF EDUCATION

DR. SAVITA MISHRA | DR. MUKTA GOYAL & MR.UDAY MODAK

Contents

Foreword

I am delighted to write this foreword because I believe deeply in the educative value of interpretive discussion for all students, especially in a democratic society. I also believe that teachers at every level and stage of their career can enrich and strengthen their teaching by learning the discussion-leading patterns and practices presented in this book. Participating in interpretive discussions can help teachers and students alike learn to use their minds with power and pleasure.

The authors has conceptualized the intellectual foundations of interpretive discussion, elaborated its distinctive pedagogy, studied its patterns and impact on teachers and students, and designed unique systems for inducting others into this powerful educational practice through the content of this book.

This book can help teachers develop a shared vision and understanding of interpretive discussion and its flexible uses across subjects and grade levels. The frame-work, annotated examples, and appendixes can structure and guide teachers' joint work as they prepare questions, co-lead discussions, observe and analyze classroom experiments, and discuss emergent questions and problems. As teachers gain confidence and skill through collaborative experimentation and development, they can also study the impact of participating in such discussions on students' confidence and academic skills.

I hope that this book will become a primer for social science researchers, teachers, teacher educators, and professional developers, helping teachers across the country to learn, teach, and practice the art of interpretive discussion.

Dr. Nandita Deb
Principal,
State Council of Educational Research and Training
(SCERT), Delhi
Government of National Capital Territory of Delhi

Preface

The book "**Learner's Psychology: Foundation of Education**" has been written with the specific purpose of providing up-to-date information and the urgent need of students studying in B.Ed, M.Ed, and B.A (Education), M.A (Education) courses and preparing for NET-JRF, SET, SLET and other competitive exams. We are confident that this book fulfills all essential requirements and its wide circulation will definitely exert an important influence on the theory of Education. In completing this self-imposed stupendous task, the authors have been quite conscious of their numerous limitations in view of the multifarious subject matter to be collected for completing this volume. Educational Psychology has been taught as a major subject in Teacher Education Programmes at different levels on the implicit assumption that knowledge of Educational Psychology gives insight into the problems of teaching-learning and develops other necessary professional skills and competencies in the progressive teachers to face the classroom teaching give the teacher much of what he needs to achieve his goals by enabling him to understand, control and predict the behavior of students. Education not only in Western countries but also in other parts of the world has been immensely influenced by the educational ideals of such great personalities. As a teacher, we felt a new interest in them and this led us to take this laborious and ambitious venture. In writing this book we have always kept in mind the interest of the students who will primarily be benefited from it. Psychologists and general readers may also get valuable information regarding the theories and practices of the Psychology of Education all over the world.

DR. SAVITA MISHRA |
DR. MUKTA GOYAL
MR.UDAY MODAK

Message

It gives me immense pleasure to announce the launch of a new publication titled "Learner's Psychology" authored by Dr. Savita Mishra, Dr. Mukta Goyal, and Mr. Uday Modak who are having experience as working professional and also experienced educator shares with us the significance of skill development for any career one opts for, which is guided by their lifelong research and hard work through this exceptional publication. I congratulate them for their sheer hard work on this exemplary accomplishment.

DR. RAJAT DEY
Principal,
Bhavan's Tripura College of Teacher Education,
Narsingarh , Agartala, Tripura.

Keywords

1. *ADOLESCENCE*
2. *ADOLESCENCE EDUCATION*
3. *ADULTHOOD*
4. *AMBIVERT*
5. *ASSESSMENT*
6. *BEHAVIORAL PROBLEMS*
7. *BEHAVIOURISM*
8. *CHILDHOOD*
9. *CHILDREN*
10. *CLASSICAL CONDITIONING THEORY*
11. *COGNITION*
12. *COMPARATIVE PSYCHOLOGY*
13. *CONDITIONING*
14. *CREATIVITY*
15. *DISRUPTIVE BEHAVIOUR*
16. *EMOTIONAL REACTION*
17. *ENTROVERT*
18. *EPISTEMOLOGY*
19. *ETHICS*
20. *HUMAN BEINGS*
21. *IDEAS*
22. *IDENTITY*
23. *INNOVATIONS*
24. *INTELLIGENCE*
25. *INTERESTS*
26. *INTROVERT*
27. *KNOWLEDGE MANAGEMENT*
28. *KNOWLEDGE*
29. *LAWRENCE KOHLBERG*
30. *LEARNER*
31. *LEARNING*
32. *MEASUREMENT*
33. *MENTALITY AND INTELLIGENCE*
34. *MORAL DEVELOPMENT*

CHAPTER ONE

CONCEPT OF EDUCATION AND PSYCHOLOGY

Introduction

The biological and societal components of human life are intertwined. While nourishment and reproduction maintain and transmit the biological part of human existence, education maintains and transmits the social aspect of human life. Because of his educable abilities, man stands out among the lower animals. He is gifted with brains, and he desires to stay active, vibrant, and even unique. The list of human accomplishments is extensive. How has all of this been accomplished? Via means of education when viewed from various angles, the concept of education resembles a diamond that appears to be of varied colours (nature) (point of view or philosophy of life).

The complex character of the human personality

- Complex nature of surroundings

- Different philosophies of life

- Different educational theories and practices are the reasons for different interpretations/definitions of education.

"The fate of India is currently being moulded in her classrooms," the Education Commission (1964-66) began its report with these lines. "The country has reached a stage in its economic and technological growth where a considerable effort must be made to reap the greatest value from the assets already developed and to ensure that the rewards of change reach all sectors," the NPE (1986) continued. Vidya / Knowledge / Learning /

Education was regarded the 'third eye' of man by ancient Indian thinkers, as it gave him insight into all situations and taught him how to act; it led to our redemption in the mundane domain, as well as all-round advancement and wealth.

Meaning of education:

The word 'education', is derived from the following Latin Words:

	Word(s) from which derived	Meaning of the word
(a)	Educatum	To train, or act of teaching or training.
(b)	Educere	To lead out, to draw out
(c)	Educare	To mould/to bring up, to raise, to educate.

www.slideserve.com

EDUCATION DEFINITION

Aristotle

Education is the process of training man to fulfill his aim by exercising all the faculties to the fullest extent as a member of society.

M.J. Langeveld

Education is every interaction that happens is every association that occurs between adults with children is a field or a state where the educational work in progress

Prof. H. Mahmud Yunus

Education efforts that are deliberately chosen to influence and assist children with the aim of improving knowledge, physical and morals that can gradually deliver the child to the highest goal.

Socrates

Education means the bringing out of the ideas of universal validity which are latent in the mind of every man.

John Dewey

Education is all one with growing; it has no end beyond itself. (Education is everything along with growth; education itself has no final destination behind him).

H.H Horne

In the broadest sense, education is the device by which a social group continued existence renew yourself, and defend his ideals

ExamPlanning.Com

examplanning.com

Psychology

Previously, psychology was considered a sub-discipline of philosophy. Psychology emerged as a separate scientific discipline when late-nineteenth-century physiologists began to examine the mind and how it functions using scientific methods.

Meaning of Psychology

In other words: Psychology is a combination of two words **psych** means **soul** and **logos** means **science**. During the development of psychology it go through different meanings like science of soul, science of mind, science of consciousness and science of behaviour.

Educational Psychology

The study of how individuals learn, including teaching methods, instructional processes, and individual differences in learning, is referred to as educational psychology. The idea is to figure out how people pick up new information and retain it.

This discipline of psychology encompasses not just the early childhood and adolescent learning processes, but also the social, emotional, and cognitive processes that are involved in learning throughout one's life.

Educational psychology research follows its beginnings to the exploratory and experimental work on affiliation and tangible movement by the English anthropologist Sir Francis Galton, and the American analyst G. Stanley Hall, who composed The Contents of Children's Minds (1883). The significant forerunner in the field of instructive brain science, notwithstanding, was the American instructor and clinician Edward Lee Thorndike, who planned techniques to quantify and test kids' knowledge and their capacity to learn. Thorndike proposed the exchange of preparing hypothesis, that's what which expresses "what is realized in one circle of movement 'moves' to another circle just when the two circles share normal 'components.' "

Educational psychology encompasses a variety of fields such as developmental psychology, behavioural psychology, and cognitive psychology.

Instructive brain science, hypothetical and exploration part of present-day brain research, worried about the educational experiences and mental issues related with the educating and preparing of understudies. The instructive clinician concentrates on the mental improvement of understudies and the different elements associated with picking up, including fitness and learning estimation, the inventive strategy, and the persuasive powers that impact elements among understudies and educators. Instructive brain research is a halfway trial and part of the way applied to part of brain science, worried about the streamlining of learning. It varies from school brain science, which is an applied field that manages issues in rudimentary and optional educational systems.

Nature of Educational Psychology

The idea of brain research in schooling is widespread as it has been acknowledged by all as a study of instruction. For the best comprehension of the idea of instructive brain science, read the focuses beneath. The idea of brain science in training is to:

1. Give information on the idea of the child
2. Give a comprehension of the nature, points and motivations behind the instruction
3. Give a comprehension of the logical techniques and strategies which have been utilized in showing up at current realities and standards of instructive brain science
4. Present the standards and methods of learning and educating
5. Give preparation in strategies for estimating capacities and accomplishment in school subjects
6. Give information on the development and improvement of youngsters
7. Aid the better change of youngsters and to assist them with forestalling maladjustment
8. Concentrate on the instructive importance and control of feelings
9. Give a comprehension of the standards and procedures of the right preparation

To summarize it, instructive brain research or brain science in schooling is an applied, positive, social, explicit and reasonable science. While general science manages the way of behaving of people in different circles, instructive brain research concentrates on the way of behaving of the person in the instructive circle as it were.

Three parts of schooling concern the instructive therapists

1. Student
2. Growing experience
3. Learning Situation

Scope Of Educational Psychology

The extent of instructive brain research is acquiring more prominent significance in the instructive field. Consequently, more understudies are planning to seek after this field of study. This makes it more significant for applicants as well as others to figure out the extent of instructive brain science. The accompanying elements show the extent of instructive brain science

1. Human Behavior

Brain research in training includes the investigation of the human way of behaving in instructive circumstances. We as a whole comprehend that brain research is the investigation of conduct. Training, then again, manages the adjustment of conduct. Thus, we can say that instructive brain science infiltrates the entire of schooling area.

2. Development and Development

How does a youngster go through different phases of development? This is concentrated by instructive analysts. The qualities of each phase of development are firmly watched and contemplated. This aids in making reports and a simple determination of a couple of sicknesses/infections.

3. Heredity and Environment

Heredity can influence a ton of things in a kid, including the turn of events and the development of the mind to learn and get a handle on new things. Alongside this, the climate a youngster experiences childhood in additionally has a significant influence. Instructive therapists decide how much heredity and climate contribute towards the development of the individual and how this information can be utilized for achieving the ideal advancement of the youngster.

4. Growing experience

Learning is a significant peculiarity in schooling. Instructive analysts concentrate on the law of learning. They concentrate on how advancing as interaction can occur successfully and monetarily. Clinicians in training comprehend how an understudy responds to learning in various circumstances

5. Character

The extent of brain research in training stretches out to the character of the understudy. It manages the nature and advancement of a person in an instructive arrangement. Instruction has been depicted as an overall advancement of the character of an individual.

6. Insight

An instructor or a coach needs to grasp the idea of the review. The extent of Psychology in schooling incorporates the investigation of the idea of knowledge as well as its estimation.

7. Individual Difference

Every individual is unique in relation to the next. This is a principal reality of human existence. Training therapist concentrates on the idea of insight as well as its estimation. This is a vital extent of brain science in schooling.

8. Direction and Counseling

At the point when you utilize the word instruction, it implies directing a developing youngster. Subsequently, direction frames a significant extent of brain science in instruction. This is one of the main fields of concentration in the subject. American Psychology Association has given five areas of direction and guidance. They are:

Human development and advancement, remembering the impact of heredity and climate for different parts of a person

The idea of the educational experience, factors impacting the growing experience

It incorporates many sub-subjects, like the emotional well-being of the understudies and educators' personality

Estimation and assessment, insights

Procedures and techniques for Educational Psychology

We can finish up by saying that instructive brain research is a smaller part of brain research. Instruction is one of the essential requirements of present day man. Brain research has advanced into each part of current schooling to make it more precise, logical, valuable, valid, evenhanded, mathematical. Solid strategies have been applied at present for the comprehension of the human brain and conduct. It had helped in working out the instructive arrangement and program for the successful arrangement of the issues.

Relationship Between Education And Psychology

(1) **Psychological and educational goals:** Educational goals can be fixed with the help of a child's psychology changes. As a result, the markers for organising any educational activity are needs, interest, aptitude, and attitude.

(2) **Psychology and curriculum:** When developing and preparing a curriculum, it is important to consider the child's developmental rate. As a result, they are complementary in the educational process.

(3) **Psychology and methods of teaching:** A teacher must offer instructions using a variety of approaches that are linked to the child's psychological problems, needs, and development.

(4) **Psychology and evaluation:** The evaluation and examination procedure as a whole should be based on psychological principles. Questions should be prepared with the children's typical development in mind. Following methods can help:

- Evaluation of child IQ (Intelligence test).
- Evaluate the factor of slow learning in the class room situation.
- Attitude and scale of intelligence test.
- The Stanford- binet scale of intelligence test.

The Stanford-Binet intelligence scale is a standardized test that assesses intelligence and cognitive abilities in children and adults aged two to twenty three years, determining the presence of a learning disability or a developmental delay.

(5) **Psychology and discipline:** Discipline issues can be addressed with the use of appropriate psychological treatments. It also aids in the detection of many behavioural issues in children.

(6) **Administration and psychology:** The administrative process should be founded on psychological techniques. Individual variances should be taken into consideration when administering.

(7) **Psychology and the teacher:** To deal with a complex educational environment, a teacher should be a master of psychology. Teaching is an art, so he should be familiar with many psychological strategies in order to solve various children's problems.

(8) **Psychology and timetables, textbook preparation:** Curriculum workers, teachers, and administrators design appropriate timetables based on the learners' interests, time, suitability, and local circumstances. Similarly, when preparing textbooks, he must consider the importance of the learner's psychological requirements, capacities, and development.

(9) **Educational Psychology and Several Phases of Growth:** An individual's personality and mental ability can be separated into different stages based on their growth, such as childhood, adolescence, and adulthood. Mental maturity is at various stages during these periods. Psychologists believe that if the reaching process is broken down into three parts, it will be much easier to learn. At different phases, different teaching

methods are used. Without a thorough understanding of psychology, this is impossible.

(10) **Educational Psychology and Personality Development:** The goal of education is to help people develop their personalities. It is impossible to analyse the stimuli and responses of personality flaws, as well as their causes and reforms, without a thorough understanding of psychology.

As a result, psychology and education have a strong relationship. Psychologies education, according to Pestalozzi. Before beginning to teach, every teacher should study about child psychology.

CHAPTER TWO

INTRODUCTION TO PSYCHOLOGY

Meanings of Psychology:
Etymologically brain research implies the study of the spirit, viz., 'psyche' means

'soul' and 'logos' signifies 'science.'
The previous analysts kept up with that the capacity of brain science was to study

the nature, beginning and the fate of the human spirit.
Current analysts, in any case, question the presence of the spirit since there is no

experimental proof for its presence.
A considerable lot of the prior therapists, notwithstanding, had confidence in the presence of the
mind.

A few contemporary clinicians likewise put stock in the presence of the psyche.

(I) Psychology is the Science of Mind:

• In 1892 William James characterized brain research as the 'study of mental processes'.

• In his view, brain research might be characterized regarding cognizant states.

(ii) Psychology is the Science of Consciousness:

• In 1884 James Sully characterized brain research as the study of the 'internal world' as

recognized from actual science which concentrate on the actual peculiarities.

• In 1892 Wilhelm Wundt characterized brain research as the science which studies the
'inner encounters'.

(iii) Psychology is the Science of Behavior:

• In 1905 William McDougall characterized brain research as the 'study of conduct'.

• In 1911 W. B. Pillsbury additionally characterized brain research as the 'study of conduct'.

• J. B. Watson, be that as it may, disposed of the ideas of the 'mind', 'cognizance', 'reason'
and so forth from mental use, and characterized brain research as 'the study of
conduct'.

**(iv) Psychology is the Science of the Experience and Behavior of the Individual in
Connection to his Environment:**

• K. Koffka holds that despite the fact that the idea of 'awareness' can't be totally
disposed of from mental jargon the primary point of brain science is the investigation of
conduct.

• R. S. Woodworth characterizes brain research as the "study of exercises of the person."

The Four Goals Of Psychology:

• The investigation of brain research has Four Goals -

1. Portray :

• Portraying things is something we do each and every day with no cognizant
thought or exertion. However, depicting in brain research has a somewhat unique importance
than the depicting we do in our regular day to day existence.

• Portraying an issue, an issue, or conduct is the main objective of brain research.

• Portrayals assist therapists with recognizing typical and unusual
conduct and gain an additional exact comprehension and viewpoint on human
also, creature conduct, activities, and contemplations.

2. Make sense of :

• Analysts are extremely keen on having the option to make sense of conduct instead of
simply having the option to depict it.
• This aides in giving solutions to inquiries concerning why individuals respond in a
certain way, why they do the things they do and the variables which influence their
character, their psychological well-being, their activities, and so forth.

3. Anticipate :
• Making forecasts about how we think, and act is the third objective of brain science. By
seeing past noticed conduct (portraying and making sense of) clinicians expect to
anticipate how that conduct will show up in the future later on and whether others
could display a similar way of behaving.
• Through the method involved with depicting a clarification, therapists can see more about what considerations, sentiments, and ways of behaving are contributing
factors.
• They can then utilize that information to anticipate why, when, and how those things
could occur from here on out.

4. Change/Control :
• Brain science intends to change, impact, or control conduct to make positive,
helpful, significant, and enduring changes in individuals' lives and to impact their way of behaving to improve things. This is the last and most significant objective of
brain research

Fast facts about psychology

• Psychology is the study of behaviour and the mind.
• There are various kinds of brain research, like mental, legal, social, and formative brain science.
• An individual with a condition that influences their psychological wellness might profit from evaluation and treatment with an analyst.
• A therapist might offer treatment that spotlights on conduct variations.

- A specialist is a clinical specialist who is bound to zero in on clinical administration of psychological well-being issues.

Branches of psychology

There are various sorts of psychology that fill various needs. There is no decent approach to ordering them, yet here are a few normal sorts.

Clinical psychology

Clinical psychology incorporates science, hypothesis, and practice to comprehend, anticipate and assuage issues with change, incapacity, and inconvenience. It advances adaption, change, and self-improvement.

A clinical analyst focuses on the scholarly person, close to home, organic, mental, social, and conduct parts of human execution all through an individual's life, across fluctuating societies and financial levels.

Clinical psychology can assist us with understanding, forestall, and reduce mentally caused misery or brokenness, and advance a singular's prosperity and self-awareness.

Psychological assessment and psychotherapy are fundamental to the act of clinical brain science, yet clinical analysts are much of the time additionally associated with research, preparing, measurable declaration, and different regions.

Cognitive psychology

Cognitive psychology examines inward mental cycles, for example, critical thinking, memory, learning, and language. It sees individuals' thought process, see, convey, recollect, and learn. It is firmly connected with neuroscience, reasoning, and etymology.

Cognitive psychologists see how individuals obtain, cycle, and store data.

Viable applications incorporate how to further develop memory, increment the exactness of navigation, or how to set up instructive projects to help learning.

Developmental psychology

This is the logical investigation of deliberate psychological changes that an individual encounters over the life expectancy, frequently alluded to as human turn of events.

It centers around babies and small kids as well as teens, grown-ups, and more seasoned individuals.

Factors incorporate coordinated abilities, critical thinking, moral grasping, gaining language, feelings, character, self-idea, and personality development.

It additionally takes a gander at inborn mental designs against learning through experience, or how an individual's attributes communicate with natural factors and how this effects advancement.

Formative brain research covers with fields like etymology.

Evolutionary psychology

Evolutionary psychology is likewise called conduct medication or clinical brain research.

It sees how conduct, science, and social setting impact disease and wellbeing.

An evolutionary psychologist frequently takes a gander at the organic reasons for an illness, however a wellbeing therapist will zero in general individual and what impacts their wellbeing status. This might incorporate their financial status, training, and foundation, and ways of behaving that might affect the sickness, like consistence with directions and medicine.

Forensic psychology

Forensic psychology involves applying psychology to criminal investigation and the law.

A forensic psychologist practices psychology as a science within the criminal justice system and civil courts.

Health psychology

Health psychology is also called behavioral medicine or medical psychology.

It observes how behavior, biology, and social context influence illness and health.

A physician often looks first at the biological causes of a disease, but a health psychologist will focus on the whole person and what influences their health status. This may include their socioeconomic status, education, and background, and behaviors that may have an impact on the disease, such as compliance with instructions and medication.

Health psychologists usually work alongside other medical professionals in clinical settings.

Neuropsychology

Neuropsychology checks out at the design and capacity of the cerebrum corresponding to ways of behaving and mental cycles. A neuropsychology might be involved assuming a condition includes injuries in the cerebrum, and evaluations that include keep electrical movement in the mind.

A neuropsychological assessment is utilized to decide if an individual is probably going to encounter social issues following thought or analyzed mind injury, like a stroke.

The outcomes can empower a specialist to give treatment that might end up being useful to the individual accomplish potential enhancements in mental harm that has happened.

Occupational psychology

Occupational psychology are engaged with surveying and making suggestions about the presentation of individuals at work and in preparing.

They assist organizations with tracking down additional successful ways of working, and to comprehend how individuals and gatherings act at work.

This data can assist with further developing viability, proficiency, work fulfillment, and worker maintenance.

Social psychology

Social psychology utilizes logical techniques to comprehend what social impacts mean for human way of behaving. It tries to make sense of how sentiments, conduct, and considerations are affected by the genuine, envisioned or inferred presence of others.

A social psychologist takes a gander at bunch conduct, social insight, non-verbal way of behaving, congruity, animosity, bias, and initiative. Social insight and social connection are viewed as key to figuring out friendly way of behaving.

Different branches incorporate military, purchaser, instructive, multifaceted, and natural brain research. The quantity of branches keeps on developing.

CHAPTER THREE

IMPORTANCE OF EDUCATIONAL PSYCHOLOGY AND ITS POPULAR THEORIES

Educational Psychology and its Importance

Introduction

Instructive brain science is committed to the review and improvement of human learning, across the life expectancy, in anything setting it happens.

Such settings incorporate schools, yet in addition working environments, coordinated sports, government organizations, and retirement networks - anyplace people are participated in guidance and learning of some sort.

Instructive brain science is significant as a result of its emphasis on understanding and working on the critical human ability to learn.

In this mission of improving learning, instructive analysts try to help understudies and educators the same.

- **A Brief History of the Field**

Instructive PsychologyAs noted above, early Greek thinkers, for example, Plato and Aristotle were worried about the educational experience, for authentic and moral information.

Notwithstanding, it was only after later in history that instructive brain science arose as a field by its own doing, particular from reasoning.

John Locke (1632-1704), the persuasive British scholar and "father of brain research," broadly depicted the human psyche as a clean slate (clean canvas) that had no intrinsic or characteristic information, however could learn through the aggregation of encounters.

Johann Herbart (1776-1841) is viewed as the pioneer behind instructive brain science as a particular field. He underscored interest in a subject as a vital part of learning.

He likewise proposed five conventional strides of learning:

1. It is as of now known to Review what
2. Seeing new material to be learned
3. Introducing new material
4. It is now known to Relate new material to what
5. Demonstrating the way that new information can be helpfully applied

Maria Montessori (1870-1952) was an Italian doctor and instructor who began by showing incapacitated and oppressed kids. She then, at that point, established an organization of schools that showed offspring of all foundations utilizing an active, multi-tactile, and frequently understudy guided way to deal with learning.

Nathaniel Gage (1917-2008) was a persuasive instructive clinician who spearheaded research on educating. He served in the U.S. Armed force during WWII, where he created fitness tests for choosing plane guides and radar administrators.

Gage proceeded to foster an exploration program that did a lot to propel the logical investigation of instructing.

He accepted that advancement in advancing exceptionally relies upon successful instructing and that a powerful hypothesis of viable instructing needs to cover:

1. The method involved with educating
2. Content to be instructed
3. Understudy capacities and inspiration level
4. Homeroom the executives

The above is just an example of the compelling masterminds who have offered over the long haul to the field of instructive brain research.

For an astounding and compact history of instructive brain science from Plato and Aristotle through behaviorism and other present day developments, if it's not too much trouble, see Grinder (1989).

- **Expected set of responsibilities and Roles of an Educational Psychologist**

Instructive clinicians have commonly procured either a graduate degree or doctorate in the field.

They work in an assortment of instructing, research, and applied settings (e.g., K-12, colleges, the military, and instructive ventures like reading material and test engineers).

Those with a doctorate frequently instruct and do explore at schools or colleges.

They show essential courses like Introduction to Educational Psychology and further developed workshops like Professional Ethics in Educational Psychology, or Research Methods in Educational Psychology.

They direct exploration on themes like the best proportion of proficiency abilities for understudies in optional schooling, the best strategy for showing early vocation experts in designing, and the connection between training level and close to home wellbeing in retired folks.

Instructive analysts additionally work in different applied jobs, for example, counseling on educational program configuration; assessing instructive projects at schools or preparing destinations; and offering educators the best informative techniques for a branch of knowledge, grade level, or populace, be it standard understudies, those with incapacities, or talented understudies.

- **Real-Life Examples**

Mamie Phipps ClarkHoward Gardner, teacher at the Harvard Graduate School of Education, is known for having fostered the hypothesis of different insights.

This hypothesis expresses that other than the customarily estimated verbal and visual-spatial types of insight, there are likewise shapes that incorporate sensation or athletic knowledge, relational or social-capacity to appreciate people on a deeper level, melodic or imaginative insight, and maybe different structures we have not yet figured out how to quantify.

Dr. Gardner instructs, conducts research, and distributes. His many books incorporate Frames of Mind: The Theory of Multiple Intelligences (1983) and The Disciplined Mind: Beyond Facts and Standardized Tests, the Education That Every Child Deserves (2000).

Mamie Phipps Clark (1917-1983), displayed above, was the main African-American lady to get a doctorate in brain science from Columbia University. She and her better half Kenneth Clark (1914-2005) were keen on improvement and confidence in African-American kids.

Her doctoral work outlined the dehumanizing impact of isolated schools on both African-American and white youngsters, in the notable "doll review" (Clark and Clark, 1939). She found that both African-American youngsters and white kids attributed more certain qualities to white dolls than to Black dolls.

This work was utilized as proof in Brown v. Leading body of Education (1954), the consistent U.S. High Court deciding that concluded that schools isolated by race were not equivalent and should be integrated.

She and her significant other established a few organizations devoted to giving guiding and instructive administrations to oppressed African-American youngsters, including the Harlem Youth Opportunities Unlimited venture.

Irene Marie Montero Gil procured her graduate degree from the Department of Evolutionary and Educational Psychology at the Autonomous University of Madrid, Spain.

Ms. Montero Gil had been offsetting ensuing doctoral examinations with her job as the most youthful individual from Spain's Congress of Deputies, addressing Madrid. She later deferred her investigations to turn into Spain's Minister of Equality, an office that supporters for equivalent open door paying little mind to progress in years, orientation, or handicap.

The above models show simply a few commitments that instructive analysts can make in research, educating, lawful, and promotion settings.

Introduction to Educational Psychology Theory

Educational psychology can influence programs, curricula, and lesson development, as well as classroom management approaches. For example, educators can use concepts from educational psychology to understand and address the ways rapidly changing technologies both help and harm their students' learning. In addition, educational psychologists play an important role in educating teachers, parents, and administrators about best practices for learners who struggle with conventional education methods.

Educational psychologists concentrate on students and learning settings — both inside and past customary homerooms — and assess manners by which factors like age, culture, orientation, and physical and social conditions impact human learning. They influence instructive hypothesis and practice in light of the most recent exploration connected with human improvement to comprehend the profound, mental, and social parts of human learning.

As psychologists, these professionals often work directly with children — and in collaboration with parents and teachers — to improve a child's learning outcomes. However, educational psychologists can also pursue careers as researchers, consultants, and teachers in a variety of contexts, including schools, community organizations, government research centers, and learning centers.

3 Popular Theories of Educational Psychology are :

Different speculations have been created to represent how people learn. The absolute most persevering and delegate cutting edge speculations are examined underneath.

1. Behaviorism

Behaviorism compares learning with perceptible changes in movement (Skinner, 1938). For instance, a sequential construction system laborer could have "learned" to collect a toy from parts, and after 10 practice meetings, the specialist can do as such without blunders in 60 seconds or less.

In behaviorism, there is an emphasis on boosts or prompts to activity (your boss gives you a container of toy parts), trailed by a way of behaving (you gather the toy), trailed by support or deficiency in that department (you get a raise for the quickest toy get together).

Behaviorism holds that the social reactions that are decidedly supported are bound to repeat from here on out.

We ought to take note of that behaviorists trust in a pre-set, outer reality that is logically found by learning.

A few researchers have additionally held that according to a behaviorist viewpoint, students are more responsive to natural improvements than dynamic or proactive in the educational experience (Ertmer and Newby, 2013).

Notwithstanding, one of the most vigorous advancements in the later behaviorist practice is that of positive conduct mediation and supports (PBIS), in which proactive procedures assume a noticeable part in improving advancing inside schools.

Such proactive conduct upholds remember expanding structure for homerooms, showing clear social assumptions ahead of time, consistently utilizing prompts with understudies, and effectively administering understudies (Simonsen and Myers, 2015).

North of 2,500 schools across the United States currently apply the PBIS steady social system, with archived upgrades in both understudy conduct (Bradshaw, Waasdorp, and Leaf, 2012) and accomplishment (Madigan, Cross, Smolkowski, and Stryker, 2016).

2. Cognitivism

Cognitivism was mostly roused by the improvement of PCs and a data handling model accepted to be material to human learning (Neisser, 1967).

It additionally grew halfway as a response to the apparent furthest reaches of the behaviorist model of realizing, which was thought not to represent mental cycles.

In cognitivism, learning happens when data is gotten, organized, held in memory, and recovered for use.

Cognitivists are distinctly keen on a neuronal or a mind to-conduct viewpoint on learning and memory. Their lines of exploration frequently incorporate examinations including practical mind imaging (e.g., utilitarian attractive reverberation imaging) to see which cerebrum circuits are actuated during explicit learning undertakings.

Cognitivists are additionally definitely keen on "brain adaptability," or how learning makes new associations be made between individual synapses (neurons) and their more extensive neuronal organizations.

According to the cognitivist viewpoint, people are seen as exceptionally dynamic in the educational experience, including how they put together data to make it by and by significant and important.

Cognitivists, similar to behaviorists, accept that learning mirrors an outside the real world, instead of forming or building reality.

3. Constructivism

Constructivism holds that from youth on, people learn in progressive stages (Piaget, 1955).

In these stages, we match our essential ideas, or "outlines," of reality with encounters on the planet and change our patterns as needs be.

For instance, in light of specific encounters as a youngster, you could shape the schematic idea that all articles drop when you let them go. However, suppose you get a helium swell that ascents when you let go of it. You should then change your pattern to catch this new reality that "most things drop when I let go of them, however no less than one thing rises when I let go of it."

For constructivists, there is generally an emotional part to how the truth is coordinated. According to this point of view, learning can't be said to mirror a pre-set outside the real world. Rather, the truth is generally an exchange between one's dynamic development of the world and the actual world.

Constructivism holds that from youth on, people learn in progressive stages (Piaget, 1955).

In these stages, we match our essential ideas, or "outlines," of reality with encounters on the planet and change our patterns as needs be.

For instance, in light of specific encounters as a youngster, you could shape the schematic idea that all articles drop when you let them go. However, suppose you get a helium swell that ascents when you let go of it. You should then change your pattern to catch this new reality that "most things drop when I let go of them, however no less than one thing rises when I let go of it."

For constructivists, there is generally an emotional part to how the truth is coordinated. According to this point of view, learning can't be said to mirror a pre-set outside the real world. Rather, the truth is generally an exchange between one's dynamic development of the world and the actual world.

CHAPTER FOUR

PSYCHOLOGY OF LEARNERS AND BETTERMENT OF LEARNER'S ATTITUDES IN LEARNING PROCESS

Introduction

It is fact that psychology deals with attitude and characters of learners in learning process. In learning process, it is mandatory for the teacher to know about the learners' personality and his family background for fruitful results from learners in learning process.

The learning of environment plays a significant role in brain development. As, adolescent performs an important mental task. The neural network that supports those abilities strengthen necessary their cognitive, emotion-regulate a memory skills. Without opportunities to use these skills, these networks remain under-developed making it challenging for individuals to engage in higher order thinker as adults.(Robyn Harper, August 2018)

In the materialistic world of mundane life, generally, prefer solution of body requirements rather than development of soul requirements. Every religion and its teachings help us to promote religious and spiritual values that make us civilized and helpful for humanity. Therefore, in learning process, both worldly and spiritual must be fulfilled for the betterment of learners. Otherwise, without spiritual and civilized education, degree may be attained in worldly institutions but the person may be manners-less after neglecting the manners and spiritual teachings of any religion of the world.

There are different types of psychologies but social psychology is that psychology which studies the behavior of mankind. But the requirements of body and soul are different while every man is compound of soul and body. The soul is invisible while body is visible. In societies, there are active and popular organizations on the basis characters of their members or employees or combination of management and members also. (Masood Tahira Dr., 2017)

Anyhow, behind any person's behavior, there are many factors that influence particular person to adopt strict or soft corner in behavior. In this, past incidents of his life, past accidents of relatives or friends and his current financial position and current friend or relatives attitudes to this particular are also.

As author of 'Social Psychology', stated that behind person's attitudes, past events effect his behavior regarding present thing.(Mughal Tariq Mahmood, 2013) In the present world, fact is that if any person is deceived by some other person of any other particular tribe or of particular department, definitely, his behavior will be bitter in future on the bases of past events about persons of this particular tribe or department. Similarly, if any learner gets good guidance and feels impressive from any institution, definitely in future, that particular person will have positive views and guides other to get admission in this institution as proposal.

Similarly, in the changing of persons' behaviors, current incidents or losses make persons bitter regarding behavior of the people of societies.(Mughal Tariq Mahmood, 2013) In societies, if you want spread positive activities then it is necessary that positive values must be encouraged and the persons who are uncivilized, these must be discouraged and their weaknesses must be pinpointed for correction not for discussion.

In educational institutions, generally, teachers' attitude about hard working students and intelligent students remain positive and mostly teachers appreciate these types of learners due to their efficacy in studies. Similarly in any organization, hardworking and efficient worker will be encouraged in the eyes of his boss. Therefore, in educational institutions such types of steps must be taken so that teacher could involve students in teaching activities. In this way, students can become hard working and civilized if regular care is done.

In learning process in schools, the teacher's behavior about the students who complete their work, will be good and favorable rather than those who do not do homework or dull in class activities. (Bhutta Waqar Ahmad, 2009) It is the duty of teachers that they should not neglect the dull students in learning activities so that they can improve their educational weaknesses. It is my practical experience that with proper care, dull and weak students are improved with the passage of time. While if these are neglected and not provided proper care, they leave their studies in early age.

Furthermore, if someone wants to change person's behaviors then by creating difficult situation about future or danger of foreign attack, changing in behavior of the people may occur.(Mansoor Ali Akbar, 1998) As in the perceptions of war, or danger of war, mostly people will increase shopping than demand due to danger of war. Similarly if educated persons are employed on heavy earnings, this will be encouragement for the present learners to study more on the hope of good paying jobs. If educated persons remain un-employed or can gain low level of income. This will be actually discouragement for present learners so that they will continue study without any interest.

Anyhow, some scholars opine that teachers can correct the behaviors of their students' attitude if they are not doing well. While some others opine that teachers cannot correct students' attitude because they favor of the given quotation, 'Nature cannot change.' Anyhow, changing of students' attitude may be improved in some students while in some students, teachers' guidance may not be improved but for very low number, this may be occurred.

Teachers cannot actually control their students' behavior. That's because the only behavior, person can control in his or her own. And when teachers try directly to restrict what say or do, they are usually left feelings frustrated and helpless. (Shari Gent, March 22, 2021)

Training of individual is crucial for the promotion of civilized society. In actual, training of individuals in present time will show its results/ outcomes in future. This is why, in every department of any country, training is provided for its employees so that particular sense might be developed.

As, Allama Asad wrote that, societies can built only in the result of trainings and polite behaviors of trainers which are used in learning manners.(Muhammad Asad Allama, March 2009) learners' attitude may be affected from the attitude of teachers or master trainers in learning or training activities. Similarly, if teachers' behavior is impressive then learners will be attracted from his style.

Similarly if teacher will use rude behavior in teaching or in learning activities, this will be dangerous for students and students will feel boredom. Therefore, learning process must be as so that learners feel happy in learning process.

And teachers can control the wrong activities of students in class by presenting such style and manner so that concerning involved student try to avoid from wrong behavior or unsuitable behavior. (Shari Gent, March 22, 2021) Besides these, if wrong behavior is not corrected by the teacher, or if teachers continue teaching activities and students remain busy in their wrong activities in class, This means both groups are just spending their time, or it may be stated that time is being killed. Therefore, it is better for fruitful results in learning for the students and for the teachers that both should take interest fully. And teachers should perform their duties having fear of God with honestly. Same is upon for learners otherwise there is need to change students attitude regarding learning.

While Edward Kang stated that, teacher can guide students to avoid ineffective studying habits in favor of ones that will increase their learning outcomes. Too often people imagine that long hours of studying are the best path to being a model straight a student. Yet research shows that highly successful students actually spend less time studying than their peers' do-they just study more effectively. (Edward Kang, April 4, 2019)

As concerned the responsibility of teachers or learners concerned, this may be stated that children are innocent so they influence from things and people at once. Therefore, teachers and parents are more responsible as they know the time, the people, about good or bad values and attitudes of the people with their effects. This may supported from Meaning of Holy Prophet's sayings that every child takes his birth in nature but it is upon his parents that make him, Muslim, Jew, Christian or follower of any other religion. The reason is that children are innocents so elders, the old and others are responsible to keep the children on track of success.

And Emma Chippa stated that students are just like agriculture and plants, as you will care the plants safe from any kinds of raw roots or grass, then they will be grow safely otherwise, there will be problem to grow safely and to become civilized. (Emma Chiappetta, June 18, 2021)

It is empirical evidence that sometimes, educated parents cannot provide better guidance and better learning institution but sometimes uneducated persons can provide better guidance and learning environment. Due to this, the children / learners of uneducated persons can achieve good marks and good values in the societies. This also refers that theoretical values are different from practical values. And for attaining good and civilized values/ manners, adoption of practical values will be useful.

While Edward Kang stated that there are following recommended techniques for high intensity study habits. These are as under:

I.   Pre-test;
II. Spaced practice;
III. Self-Quizzing;
IV. Inter-learning practice;
V.   Paraphrasing & Reflecting.[xii] (Edward Kang, April 4, 2019)

For fruitful learning and better techniques, the learner must involve himself in studying activities. And for preparation of any test, learner must analyze himself by self-test before taking any test so that he can remove mistakes and shortcoming before the actual test time. The advantage of pre-test activities will be useful as it will provide chance to paraphrase the sentences.

In Amin's views, habits become nature when actions are repeated again and again. (Muhammad Amin Dr., 2004). In classes, it is duty of teachers and in homes; it is duty of parents that they must know about actions of their young ones so that proper solution for these actions must be proposed.

Without considering this, this habit is useful or not useful, or this habit is good for individuals or for societies. In learning institutions, it is the duty of teacher and management of institutions to provide better conditions for learning activities so that learner can adopt positive and cultured values.

The fact is that sociologists opine that the purpose of social and welfare organizations is to provide satisfaction to humanity regarding their needs. Therefore, mostly organizations are established especially for the promotion of availability of basic needs without considering, caste, creed and color. (Bhutta Waqar Ahmad, 2009)

In a comprehensive report about madaris, it is presented that these are spreading mostly positive values besides these, some are promoting particular school of thought which is against unity of Muslim. (Editor/ compiler, 1988) In an analysis about religious madaris of different countries, it is known that religious madaris are more fruitful regarding religious education or for preparation of hereafter life rather than worldly or mundane life of Muslims. But formal and non-formal institutions are preparing just for mundane life rather than hereafter life. Therefore, it may be stated that present scenario, for Muslims, from educational institutions, madaris are more useful than formal schools or colleges or universities only for religious activities and religious education. But the drawback of madaris is that, in this separate school of thought is stressed rather than remain united even within the Muslims. Similarly, in Hindus, or Christians, separate education is provided regarding their religions.

Here, it may be stated that worldly education and the religious education has been divided in different categories among all religion in present era. This is why, educated of one particular school of thought has different point of view about the educated and qualified person of other school of thought or religion. This is the main base of discrimination among the scholars of different institutions in different countries of the world.

It is reality that if you want to know about the level of civilization of any society, or any nation, then from the level of crimes, it may be analyzed that this society or nation is civilized or not. If crimes ratio is low, it refers that people are civilized and these are busy in learning and positive activities.

In Rehman's views those societies promote and become popular in which negative actions and values are discouraged while good values are encouraged by the individuals and by the societies without considering its results. (Rehman Khalid, 2010)

It may be stated from Rehman's views that good qualities and values notify about the level and standard of society. In any society, crimes are increasing and culprits are not sentenced. This refers that in this society, wrong activities are not discouraged or justice system is not working properly. The reason of increasing crime is also easiness and shirking behavior from hardworking. Therefore, such steps must be taken for learners in the institutions so that they could do their work in taking interest and with hard working. Hard working ability will be useful in all the sectors of life in future.

In Saleem's views success is in the hardworking. Those nations become the habitual of hardworking, one day or next day, they can become to see their success. (Khalid saleem Mansoor, 2003) From Saleems' views, it may be stated that from learners' activities, it may be stated that learner will become successful nation in future or not, If the learners of any nation are hard working in their activities, this refers to identify that these learners will soon attain their goal whatever they have set it in their minds. The reason is that it is famous quotation that hardworking is the key to success.

History also shows that great scholars and scientists and great leaders of the world all have common quality/ability i.e. hardworking. With the help of hardworking ability or habit, learners can achieve their goals as intelligent can achieve.

In Shahab's views, as concerned the difference of learning is just like the difference of Muslims' actions.(Shahab Qudratullah, 2004) As concerned Shahab's views, he want say that learning process in different institutions is different because of practical role of teachers/ Muslims. Here, it may be stated that learners are influence from the person they are being provided learning activities. Therefore if a teacher is practical Muslim or practical Hindus or of other religion, then learners will be more attractive from his activities than that person who is not good in his character whether he is a Muslim or Non-Muslim. It may be derived that teacher's role has also influence to the learners. Besides teachers' role, schools/ institutions and management role are not neglect able.

In Monique's point of view, schools can play an important role in adolescents' identity development. No doubt, all adolescents are not same. There are three types of groups of adolescents regarding their abilities.(Monique Verhoeven, Astrid Mita poortuis & Monique Volman, March, 2019) It is fact that the role of schools, colleges or universities may be impressive for learners if its management provide complete facilities to the learners and learning activities are done without wasting time. In this type of institutions, students' knowledge will increase and student will feel satisfaction in the core of their hearts. And these students will become the advertiser of this particular school/college/ university/ institution. Otherwise, student will not consider good about this institution.

Concluding Remarks

In nutshell, it may be stated that learning activities must be impressive for the learners so that it may guide dull and weak learners separately with special care. In learning activities, teachers' role or role of master trainer cannot be ignored. Furthermore, learners' role and their attitude may be changed if some are not taking interest in learning activities. Teachers and the mater trainers also keep in mind that their attitude also must be for the betterment of learners rather than not just for spending time. No doubt, learners' and trainers' attitude regarding values and manners must be ideal otherwise All these activities and trainer's words will not be fruitful for leaners if he is offering words only from mouth rather than core of hearts. Anyhow, with worldly education, religious education must be provided to the learners of particular religion that will create emotions to help humanity. Any teachers/ trainers must keep in mind, the sociological status and economic condition of learners so that they could behave them in light of condition which will be useful in learning process.

CHAPTER FIVE

UNDERSTANDING THE DEVELOPMENTAL CHARACTERISTICS OF THE LEARNER

Concept of Development

The Learning Objective's Concept is the overarching notion or generalization. You directly teach the concept, what it is, the generalization, and the major idea to the pupils in Concept Development. A documented, ironclad definition, as well as examples and non-examples, are included in the Concept (if applicable). The Learning Objective should be the source of the Concept. In the Learning Objective, it is frequently the noun:

Example:

- Make inferences based on the information provided in the text.
- Calculate a rectangular prism's volume.
- Describe the mitotic process.
- Describe the United States Constitution's checks and balances.

Although most concepts are nouns, some, like Add numbers to 10 using objects, can be verbs. In this situation, the concept or main idea is that adding means figuring out how much you have in total.

What is Included in Concept Development?

A bulletproof definition or rule containing the concept's important qualities must be included in the Concept. Exercising the concept by disclosing essential, non-critical, and shared attributes, examples and non-examples (if applicable) are offered. To emphasise those qualities, examples are presented. Non-examples aid in the clarification of the idea or demonstrate how some of the concept's characteristics are frequently shared with other concepts.

A concept has properties that are critical, non-critical, and shared.

- The presence of critical qualities is unavoidable.
- At times, non-critical properties are present. To provide clarity or further information about a concept, additional statements or phrases may be required.
- Other notions can share similar properties. To prevent pupils from overgeneralizing, it's critical to demonstrate them how qualities are related to other concepts.

Why is Concept Development Relevant?

The importance of concept development can be summed up as follows:

1. Concept development is crucial since it requires the instructor to have a clear understanding and explanation of what is being taught, as well as a written reference for students, particularly English Learners.
2. Students need to develop concepts so that they can generalise new situations in school and in real life. Students require a strong conceptual foundation before they can apply what they've learned to new situations. Students, for example, can calculate how much paint is needed to paint a wall since they realise that determining area is involved.
3. Concept development is necessary so that students can internalise the generalisation rather than learning specific examples. Teach the rule that Days of the Week are usually capitalised, for example. Instead of teaching pupils about individual days, this is a generic guideline that they may apply to any day of the week. According to brain studies (Allard 2007), in order for knowledge to be kept in long-term memory, it should be delivered in generalizations (one hook) rather than specific examples (many random hooks). Students' information is not stored in long-term memory if they are not taught concepts.
4. Because all students should be able to express the topics being taught, concept development is important. According to Richard Clark, Paul

Kirschner, and John Sweller's paper Putting Children on the Path of Learning, students with no relevant concepts in long-term memory will hunt for solutions blindly for long periods of time and learn absolutely nothing.

5. State examinations and Common Core Assessments are used to assess concepts. The notion primary idea in the question is used in the 5th grade Smarter Balanced Assessment, for example. In order to select the proper answer, students will need to understand what the key idea is.

Principles of Growth & Development and their Educational Implication

Introduction: -

Concepts are assessed through state exams and Common Core Assessments. The principal idea of the question, for example, is used in the 5th grade Smarter Balanced Assessment. Students will need to understand the essential notion in order to choose the correct answer.

Meaning of Growth: -

State tests and Common Core Assessments are used to evaluate concepts. In the 5th grade Smarter Balanced Assessment, for example, the question's main premise is employed. In order to choose the proper answer, students must first grasp the fundamental concept.

Definition: -

Arnold Gessel claims that "Rather than the environment, growth is a function of the organism. The environment provides the soil and surroundings for development manifestations, but these manifestations are the result of an inherent, inner organism and an intrinsic development physiology. Growth is such a complex and delicate process that it necessitates strong stabilising mechanisms, as well as an inherent balance in the overall pattern and direction of the growth trend."

Meaning of Development: -

Overall changes in shape, form, or structure are referred to as development. Development is a lifelong and ongoing process. It begins with the birth of a kid and concludes with the individual's death. The term "development" refers to the changes that occur in an organism as a whole, rather than the changes that occur in individual sections.

Definition: -

Development psychology is concerned with the study of behavioural changes across time. It refers to a process in which a person's growth and capabilities vary throughout time as a result of maturation and interaction with the environment.

Principles of Growth and Development: -

* **Principle of community:**

Community development is a result of community development. It never stops from the womb to the tomb. Every person develops his or her body and mind from the moment he or she is born.

* **Principle of Individual differences:**

Individual variations in development are unaffected. Each youngster develops at his or her own pace.

* **Principle of orderly development:**

The process of development progresses from broad to specific. The youngster first learns general information before moving on to detailed or specific information.

* **Uniformity of pattern:**

Although development does not occur at the same rate for everyone and differs significantly from one person to the next, it does follow a predictable pattern.

* **Principle of interaction and maturation and learning:**

Maturation and learning both contribute to growth and development. Maturation refers to changes in a developing organism, whereas learning refers to behavioural changes.

* **Principle of unique development:**

Individuals differ in terms of their time patterns, e.g., all children start sitting up, crawling, and standing up at the same time.

- **Principle of differential development:**

There is a principle that male and female children develop differently. In comparison to boys, girls mature earlier.

- **Principle of inter- related development:**

The process of development is holistic. His physical, intellectual, emotional, social, and other types of growth are all intertwined and dependent on one another.

Educational Implication

For parents, instructors, and educators, understanding the principles of growth and development is extremely important and beneficial. The following are some examples of how growth and development principles might be applied: -

- **Adjusting school program: -**

It assists the instructor in adapting the school programme, procedures, and practices to the child's level of development, allowing him to become more productive in the classroom.

- **Sympathetic Handling: -**

It assists parents and teachers in treating their children or students sympathetically and realistically solving their difficulties.

- **Effective guidance: -**

It assists the instructor in treating the right guidance programme by allowing the teacher to grasp the individual differences of the pupils.

- **Importance of childhood period: -**

It assists parents and teachers in comprehending the significance of the childhood era. As a result, parents and instructors should provide a wide range of social and emotional experiences for their children.

- **Right expectation: -**

Its knowledge enables us to anticipate what to expect from an individual child in terms of physical, mental, and social development at various phases of development.

- **Importance of environment: -**

It aids parents and teachers in understanding and instilling the value of heredity and a healthy environment, as well as assisting us in paying proper attention to environmental conditions.

Characteristics of Development

The following are some of the most essential development characteristics:

- **Development as a continuous process: -**

The process of growth and development begins at conception and continues until the individual reaches adulthood. It progresses at a steady but steady pace rather than in leaps and bounds. Both physical and mental features develop progressively until they achieve their ultimate potential.

- **Development proceeds from general to specific response: -**

To begin with, a child's response or reactions are of a generic type. He uses his entire body to react to the circumstance and external inputs. He gradually develops distinct answers. This is true not only of his bodily responses, but also of his cognitive and emotional responses. A child's reactions, which are initially general in character, later become more specific. This is an indication of maturation and growth.

- **The development follows a pattern: -**

Development takes place in a systematic and sequential manner. Thus, the sequence of human development is infancy, early childhood, later childhood, adolescence, and adulthood.

- **A different aspect of growth develops at different stages: -**

Despite the fact that development is a continual process, the rate of growth is not consistent. As a result, there are times of rapid growth and periods of slow growth. The pace of growth slows throughout the first three years of life, but accelerates again during the adolescent stage. Similarly, not all areas of the body grow at the same rate, and not all aspects of mental development evolve at the same rate. As a result, they mature at various times.

- **Most traits are correlated in development: -**

In general, it has been assumed that a child with above-average intellectual development is also exceptional in many other areas, such as health, sociability, and unique aptitudes. Similarly, his mental development is intertwined with his physical development.

- **Development is a product of the interaction of the organism and environment: -**

Neither genes nor the environment alone is responsible for an individual's development. Both are responsible for human growth and development, while it is impossible to say exactly how much genetics and environment play a role in an individual's development.

- **Growth is both quantitative and qualitative: -**

As a child develops physically, he also develops qualitatively in terms of his personality. That is to say, when a youngster grows older, his mental and emotional functions develop as well. As a result, these two qualities are inextricably linked.

Cognitive development

Cognitive development is the process through which a person perceives, thinks about, and comprehends his or her environment as a result of the interaction of hereditary and learned elements. Information processing, intelligence, reasoning, language development, and memory are all components of cognitive development.

It was long thought that infants lacked the ability to comprehend or develop complex concepts, and that they would stay cognitively deficient until they learnt to speak. From the moment they are born, newborns are aware of their surroundings and interested in exploring them. Babies begin to actively learn from the moment they are born. They gather, sort, and interpret data from everywhere around them, then use it to improve their perceptual and reasoning abilities.

Piaget's theory of development: -

The theory of cognitive development developed by French scientist Jean Piaget (1896–1980) is the most well-known and influential. Piaget's hypothesis, initially published in 1952, was based on decades of detailed observation of children in their natural circumstances, including his own, as opposed to behaviorists' laboratory trials. Piaget was concerned in how children reacted to their surroundings, but he proposed a more active role for them than learning theory predicted. He saw a child's knowledge as being made up of schemas, which he defined as "fundamental units of knowledge used to organize past experiences and provide a foundation for understanding future ones."

Assimilation and accommodation, two complimentary processes identified by Piaget, are constantly changing schemas. Assimilation is the process of assimilating new data by incorporating it into an existing schema. To put it another way, humans assimilate new experiences by linking them to previous experiences. Accommodation, on the other hand, occurs when the schema itself changes to accommodate new information. Piaget defined cognitive development as a constant effort to achieve equilibration, which he defined as a balance between assimilation and accommodation.

Infancy: -

Infants learn to utilize their senses to investigate the world around them as soon as they are born. Most babies can focus on and follow moving objects, recognize pitch and loudness of sound, see all colors and discern hue and brightness, and begin anticipating events such as sucking at the sight of a nipple. Infants can remember faces, reproduce facial emotions such as smiling and frowning, and respond to familiar sounds by the age of three months.

Babies are just six months old when they begin to comprehend how the world works. They copy sounds, like hearing their own voice, recognize their parents, avoid strangers, distinguish between animate and inanimate objects, and measure distance based on object size. They also understand that if they drop an object, they can retrieve it. Babies can recognize their names between the ages of four and seven months.

Toddlerhood: -

Toddlers have achieved the "sensorimotor" stage of Piaget's theory of cognitive development, which involves rudimentary reasoning, between the ages of 18 months and three years. For example, they can recognize the permanence of items and people, follow the displacement of objects visually, and use instruments and equipment. Toddlers begin to seek greater independence, which can provide difficulties for parents concerned about their children's safety. They also comprehend discipline and what constitutes appropriate and inappropriate behavior, as well as the meanings of phrases such as "please" and "thank you."

Preschool: -

Preschoolers, ages three to six, should be in Piaget's cognitive development theory's "preoperational" stage, which means they are using their imagery and memory skills. They should be taught to study and memories, and their worldview is typically quite self-centered. Preschoolers have often developed social interaction abilities, such as playing and cooperating with other kids their age. It's typical for preschoolers to push their cognitive capacities to their limits, and they pick up on bad concepts and behaviors like talking back to adults, lying, and bullying. Preschoolers' cognitive development also includes increasing their attention span, learning to read, and forming disciplined routines, such as doing housework.

School age: -

Younger school-age children, ages six to twelve, should be at the "concrete operations" stage of Piaget's cognitive development theory, which is characterized by the ability to think and solve problems through logical and coherent actions. They grasp the principles of permanence and conservation by understanding that despite changes in external appearance, volume, weight, and numbers can remain constant. These kids should be able to draw on their previous experiences to explain why certain things happen. Their attention span should improve as they become older, going from about 15 minutes at age six to an hour at age nine.

Adolescents between the ages of 12 and 18 should be in Piaget's "formal operations" stage of cognitive development. It is characterized by a greater ability to think through problems and circumstances on one's own. Pure abstractions, such as philosophy and higher math concepts, should be understandable to adolescents. Children should be able to learn and use general information to adapt to specific situations at this age. They should also be able to learn the specialized knowledge and abilities required for a particular job. A cognitive transition is an important part of the adolescent experience. Adolescents think in ways that are more mature, efficient, and complex than children's thinking. There are five ways to look at this talent.

CHAPTER SIX

GROWTH AND DEVELOPMENT

Introduction

The term growth implies on addition or increase in the bodily aspects that can be measured, for example, height, weight, size, muscles and length. It is best on biological processes that naturally occur over a period of time and relatively not or less influenced by context except for extreme illness or undernourishment. It eventually stops when the body parts reach the peak of their growth. While growth refers to the physical charges that an individual undergoes, development refers to certain charges that occur conception till death. It not only involves growth, but also entails disintegration and eventually decay. However, not all changes are considered as development. Rather, it applies to those changes that appear in orderly ways and are considerably permanent.

Growth vs Development in Psychology

" Psychology" is characterized as "the logical investigation of the mind and behavior.." In this discipline, it likewise covers the Growth vs Development of people. People are exceptionally intriguing subjects. People are a secret and continually change. This incorporates their development and improvement as intriguing region of this subject. "Growthand Development " generally come two by two. Yet, what are actually the distinctions among development and advancement in the area of Psychology? Allow every one of us to find out in this article.

For a quick differentiation about growth and development, psychology defines "growth" as "the physical change that a particular individual undergoes." On the other hand, psychology defines "development" as "the overall growth of humans throughout their lifespan." Development includes the understanding of how and why people change in terms of physical growth, intellectual, emotional, social, and other aspects of human growth. In psychology, there are several principles concerning growth and development. Just by looking at its principles, we can tell the differences between growth and development in psychology.

Concerning development, it generally follows an example. development is definitely not a turbulent and quick interaction. It requires investment, very much like growth. For instance, cephalocaudal succession is an example of development. Whenever a child develops, his exercises create from head to toe. A child figures out how to move his head first before he can walk. Since it follows an example, we can say that development is likewise unsurprising.

We can say that advancement is progressive and is equivalent to growth. Like development, growth is certainly not a prompt cycle. It is a ceaseless cycle. The pieces of the body ceaselessly develop given the appropriate nourishment it needs. Until the pieces of the body arrive at their pinnacle of growth, they will growing.

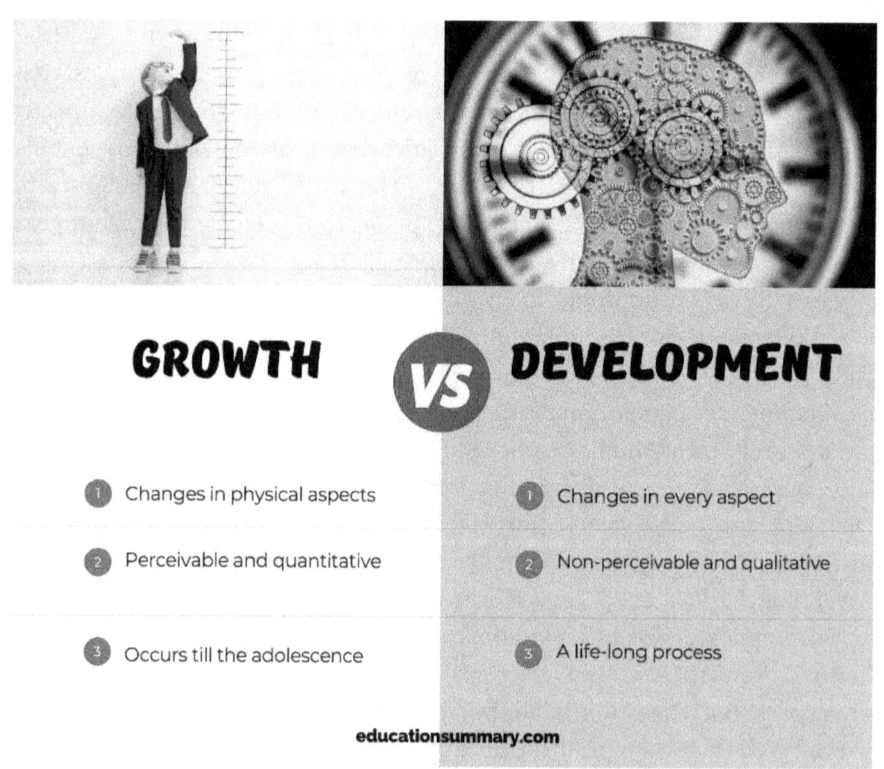

educationsummary.com

rinciples of Growth and Development

Growth and development are inseparable but they different from each other. The growth represents the physical changes of an individual and development represents the overall changes, structure and shape of an individual. Knowledge of the growth and development at the various stage is very essential for the teacher. The teacher has to stimulate the growth and development of a child. He can do it only if he has proper knowledge of the growth and development at various stage.

- **Principle of Continuity:**

The development follows the principle of Continuity which means that **development is a continuous process. It starts with pre-natal and ends with death.**

- **Principle of Integration:**

Development thus involves a movement from the whole to parts and from parts to the whole and this way it is the integration of the whole and its parts as well as the specific and general responses. It enables a child to develop satisfactorily in relation to various aspects or dimension of his personality.

Example: Child first starts to learn hand movement finger movement and then learn the movement of both hand and finger together this is called integration.

- **Principle of lack of uniformity in the Developmental rate:**

Development through the continuous process, but does not exhibit steadiness and uniformity in terms of the rate of development in various development of personality or in the developmental periods and stage of life.

Example: A person may have a high rate of growth and development in term of height and weight but may not have the same pace of mental and social development.

- **Principle of Individual difference:**

Every organism is a distinct creation in itself. One of the most important principals of development is that involves individual differences. There is no fixed rate of development. That all children will learn to walk is universal, but the time at which each child takes his her first step may vary.

- **Principle of uniformity pattern:**

Although develop does not proceed at a uniform rate and shows marked individual differences with regard to the process and outcome of various stages of development, yet it follows a definite pattern in one or the other dimension which is uniform and universal with respect to the individual of a species.

- **Principle of proceeding from general to specific:**

While developing in relation to any aspect of personality. **The child first pickup or exhibit general response and learn how to show specific and goal – directed responses afterwards.**

- **Principle of interaction between Heredity and Environment:**

Development of a child is a process that cannot be defined wholly based on either on **heredity**

Or environment. Both have to play an important role in development. There are arguments in favour of both. However, most of the psychologist agree that an interplay these two factors leads to development.

Where heredity decides or set some limits on development (mostly physical), environmental influences complete the developmental process (qualitative). Environmental influences provide space for multidimensional development through interaction with family, peers, society and so on. **Growth and development is a joint product of heredity and environment.**

- **Principle of interrelation:**

Various aspects or dimension of one's growth and development are interrelated. What is achieved or not achieved in on or other dimension in the course of the gradual and continuous process of the development surely affects the development of other dimensions?

A healthy body tends to develop a healthy mind and an emotionally stable, physically strong and socially conscious personality. Inadequate physical or mental development may, on the other hand, result in a socially or emotionally maladjusted personality.

- **Principle of Cephalocaudal:**

Development proceeds in the direction of the longitudinal axis.**Development from head to foot or toe.** That is why, before it becomes able to stand, the child first gains control over his head and arms and then on his legs.

- **Principle of proximodistal:**

Development of motor skills to Start at **Central body parts to outwards.** That is why, in the beginning, the child is seen to exercise control over the large fundamental muscles of the arm and then hand and only afterwards over the smaller of the fingers.

- **Principle of predictability:**

Development is predictable, which means that with the help of the uniformity of pattern and sequence of development. We can go to a great extent, forecast the general nature and behaviour of a child in one or more aspects or dimension at any particular stage of it's growth and development. We can know the particular age at which children will learn to walk, speak and so on.

- **Principle of Spiral versus Linear advancement:**

The child doesn't proceed straight or linear on the path of development at any stage never takes place with a constant or steady pace. After the child had developed to a certain level, there is likely to be a period of rest for consolidation of the developmental progress achieved till then. In advancing further, therefore, the development turn back and then moves forward again in a **spiral pattern.**

- **Principle of Association of Maturation and Learning:**

Biological growth and development are known as **Maturation.** Biological changes involve changes in the brain and the nervous system, which provide new abilities to a child. **Development proceeds from simple to complex.** In the beginning, a child learns through concrete objects and gradually moves to abstract thinking. This transition happens because of maturation.

Characteristics of Growth and Development:

Characteristics of Growth:

- It refers to an increase in size, length, height and weight.
- It is a function of an organism.
- It is intrinsic development.
- It follows direction and pattern.
- It does not continues throughout life. It stops after maturity.
- It refers to changes that can be quantified and measured in absolute terms.
- It is irreversible.
- It is a gradual process rather than saltatory.
- It is not uniform all through life.
- It may or may not bring development.

Characteristics of Development:

- It refers to overall changes in an organism.
- It continues throughout life.
- It implies improvement in functioning and behaviour.
- It brings qualitative changes, which are difficult to be measured directly.
- It is measured in relative terminal.
- It is reversible.
- It is determined by both heredity and environment.
- Development is also possible without growth.

Stages of Development:

It is useful to conceive of developmental periods, each Characterized by certain tasks to be accomplished. The failure to accomplish these developmental tasks is evidence of disease, either past or present.

Infancy:

At birth the infant is largely a reflex being equipped with primitive reflexes. Some of these, such as the rooting and sucking reflexes, are obviously utilitarian. It is generally true that most of the developmental milestones are first present in reflex from and then are modified as the developing central nervous system achieves peripheral connection through myelinization of the long spinal tracts. For example, the newborn infant has a firm reflex grasp. It requires about 4 months for the child to be able to reach out and seemed an object and then this is done only in a gross fashion, using chiefly the ulnar musculature. It will require another 2 months to be able to release an object held in the grasp; hence the ability to move an object from one hand to the other marks the middle of the first year. At about 9 to 10 months, thumb and finger apposition come into play, and the child becomes prehensile.

Development follows the principle of Cephalol –caudal differentiation as can easily be observed in the child's struggles to seize objects before the hand can be made to do the brains wishes. Social interplay, a cortical function, is well developed by 6 months when the child can just begin to move objects from hand to hand (shoulder girdle and cervical spine) and cannot yet usefully move the lower extremities (lumbar plexus and associated myotomes). Early speech sounds appear before ambulation is well established.

Evaluation of the very young sick infant is quite difficult because so few signs indicating disease are manifest. The social smile, the earliest sign of interpersonal interaction, appears only after about 4 weeks. Lack of even this rudimentary sign to aid an overall estimate of severity of illness commonly dictates that infants of lesser age be observed under hospital conditions until it becomes clear that no serious disease is present. Acquiring command of one's body is the major task of the first year.

Childhood:

Soon after the end of the first year, ambulation is well established. The newfound ability to leave mother ushers in the period known to most parents as the "terrible twos." The developmental task of this period is to discover and establish self- identity. For this reason, the child finds it difficult to accede to adult requests. It is essential to be established as an autonomous individual. Therefore the child cannot be agreeable, for if he or she always does the bidding of others, the fact of autonomous existence would not be firmly established. This is why it is usually futile for the examiner to try to coax a child of this age into cooperation. Firm, gentle mastery is more effective and more humane: the emerging personality is not required to lose face by yielding. Once the child has established independent existence, usually about the age of 3 years, he or she will become a friendly, amiable patient and will readily cooperate with all reasonable, nonthreatening requests.

Exploration of the environment and the interpersonal difficulties encountered with adults operate to make accident, trauma, and child abuse major health problems of this age group. Immunologic adaptations have also been changing. The young infant has certain passively acquired defenses against infectious disease that are lost toward the end of the first year. The effective replacement of this with artificial immunity and the supervision of the natural acquisition of disease resistance are major medical tasks. Until the newborn infant has lived with a recently acquired gut Flora for a while, the enteric organisms are an important hazard. The child's inability to respond to certain antigens results in vulnerability to encapsulated bacteria of the respiratory tract for the first few years, creating a spectrum of disease unique to this time of life.

Acquiring the skills for independent function within the family is the task of the next 3 years. Such things as toilet training, self- dressing, and eating behaviour are learned, and the difficulties encountered in this process are the common problems of life. Success in this phase is preparation for the next 10 years or so during which the task is to develop the capacity and skills necessary to function in our society. During these years society takes a leading role through its formalized training programs established for the young. Although the child is relatively free of acute disease, it is in these years that the slippage due to mental slowness, learning disability, chronic disease, and socioeconomic status begins to be manifest and to wreak it's secondary tolls.

Adolescence:

Adolescence, ushered in by the undeniable physiologic and anatomic changes of puberty, is Characterized by accelerating growth rates of the mesenchymal and reproductive tissues. These changes occur in females about 2 years earlier than in males. This growth spurt contains within itself, by endocrine feedback mechanisms, the seeds of its own termination. The wide range of normal developmental schedules requires great precision in descriptive terminology. To descriptive genitalia as "infantile" might be acceptable at an earlier age but will be entirely useless during this period when one normal 12 - year- old may be "infantile" and another " well developed." Tanner (1965) has described a staging of development that correlates the events of sexual development with the growth- rate curve and makes possible a quick and accurate recording of an individual's status. The use of Tanner staging is now the standard for this purpose.

The first task of adolescence is acceptance of a new body and the gender role that accompanies it. For many, this is a difficult task, one that must be approached gradually. Unisex clothing and other strategies useful in delaying the decisions required by development will be seen. Girls will be ladies one day and tomboys the next. The quiet boy who has difficulty taking on " macho" ways will be distressed. Normal differences in breast and genital size, even through temporary, cause problems.

The second task is separation from home and family and establishing oneself as an independent adult in the society. This is just as important as separating from mother was at the age of 2 and can be equally unpleasant. It is difficult for parents to understand. It is difficult for parents to understand that by being parents they are disqualified as counselors for their own children, that there must be, at least symbolically, a revolution by which their child declares his or her independence, and that after this is accomplished, their relationship, however close,must be as adult to adult and not parent to child. The necessary separation does not come easy, and the child must seek a secure base outside the home; hence the importance of peer groups and the following of styles and fads and other means of allying with resources outside the home. The essence of these is that they must differ from those of the parent generation. Parents' efforts to join their adolescent children in these pursuits in ill- conceived attempts to be "buddies" are counterproductive. Unfortunately, this failure on the part of parents to understand normal development often leads the younger generation to adopt extreme tactics such as drug abuse, running away, or pregnancy to establish the point that must be made.

For females, the menarche is the best clinical sign that the patient has entered the last phase of declining rate of growth. Males will not enter this phase until 3 or 4 years later, and the event lacks such a clear clinical marker in their case. This cessation of growth marks a logical end of pediatrics, which by current convention is usually taken to be around age 18. For practical reasons, most pediatricians use high school graduation as a convenient marker, extending it in the case of patients suffering from marked developmental delay. This practice, of course, brings the pediatrician problem of gynecology, contraception, an occasional example of non- insulin- dependent diabetes mellitus (mature – onset diabetes of the young) and other problems more Characteristics of adult practice.

Conclusion:

Continual change is the essence of life. The cessation of growth at the end of adolescence is not the end of development. Development of physical prowess, skill, and mental process continues for many years. Even middle age does not interrupt development. Inevitably a process of involution begins. Like growth in earlier years, it affects different tissues and structures at different rates, slowed at first by the replacement of declining functions with newfound skills and bionic parts. Ultimately, however, change ceases – life ceases.

And so it is that no two patients with the same diagnosis have the same disease. Their problem formulations will be different, and their appropriate Management's cannot be the same.

Summary:

"Growth" and "development" always come in pairs. Psychology defines "growth" as "the physical change that a particular individual undergoes."

Psychology defines "development" as "the overall growth of humans throughout their lifespan." Development includes the understanding of how and why people change in terms of physical growth, intellectual, emotional, social, and other aspects of human growth.

CHAPTER SEVEN

CONCEPT AND TYPES OF PERSONALITY

Introduction:

Personality is the product of social interaction in group life. In society every person has different traits such as skin, color, height and weight. They have different types of personalities because individuals are not alike. It refers to the habits, attitudes as well as physical traits of a person which are not same but have vary from group to group and society to society, everyone has personality, which may be good or bad, impressive or unimpressive. It develops during the process of socialization in a culture of a specific group or society. One cannot determine it of an individual exactly because it varies from culture to culture and time to time. For example, a killer is considered criminal in peace time and hero in war. The feeling and actions of an individual during interaction moulds the personality. It is the sum of total behaviors of the individual and covers both overt and covert behaviors, interests, mentality and intelligence. It is the sum of physical and mental abilities and capabilities.

Personality has been derived from the Latin word "persona" which means "mask" used by the actors to change their appearance. It is the combination of an individual thoughts, characteristics, behaviors, attitude, idea and habits.

Definition of Personality:

- **Macionis** define as "It is the constant pattern of thinking, feeling and acting."
- **Ogburn and Nimkoff** define it as the totality of sentiments, attitudes, idea, habits, skills and behaviors of an individual."

- Trait-based personality theories, such as those defined by **Raymond Cattell,** define personality as the traits that predict a person's behavior.
- **Brinkerhoff** defines personality as the unique attributes and abilities of the individual.
- Dewy and Humber look at personality as the way by which the individual is interrelated through ideas, actions, and attitudes to the many non- human aspects of his/her environment and biological heritage.
- Personality defines as the structures inside a person that explain why he or she creates a particular impression on others (MacKinnon, 1969).
- Personality defines as a stable set of characteristics and tendencies that determine commonalities and differences in people's behavior (James, 1994).

Characteristics of Personality:

The word personality itself stems from the Latin word persona, which refers to a theatrical mask worn by performers in order to either project different roles or disguise their identities. At its most basic, personality is the characteristic patterns of thoughts, feelings, and behaviors that make a person unique. It is believed that personality arises from within the individual and remains fairly consistent throughout life. The important roles as well as the following fundamental characteristics of personality:

- **Consistency:** There is generally a recognizable order and regularity to behaviors. Essentially, people act in the same ways or similar ways in a variety of situations.
- **Psychological and physiological:** Personality is a psychological construct, but research suggests that it is also influenced by biological processes and needs.
- **Behaviors and actions:** Personality not only influences how we move and respond in our environment, but it also causes us to act in certain ways.
- **Multiple expressions:** Personality is displayed in more than just behavior. It can also be seen in our thoughts, feelings, close relationships, and other social interactions.

Types of Personality:

Personality is those qualities through which you present yourself in front of others, these are such qualities that decide your reaction on an action of a person. It covers everything of an individual, for example walking, talking, treating and handling problems. It is a tool that measures the confidence of an individual. There are three types of personalities explained by sociologist they are:-

- Entrovert
- Introvert
- Ambivert

1. Extrovert Personality:

This type has the tendency to live mostly outside the like to live with others. Those individuals are highly socialized and have contact with outside people in the society. They want to join other groups who are more in number. These type of people are drivers, excessive drinkers, smokers, robbers, thieves, wicked persons etc.

2. Introvert Personality:

Introvert is opposite to extrovert. Those people are always live alone in their rooms and do not want to go outside. They have their own imaginary world. They are teachers, scientists, thinkers and philosophers.

3. Ambivert Personality:

Between extrovert and introvert personalities there is a third one type called ambivert. People belonging to this type enjoy both the groups and attend them. They have middle mind and want to live in both parties. Sometimes they join outside people but sometimes they live in their own rooms.

Understanding the four different personality types

It's important to understand that everyone can be categorised based on the behaviour and personality traits they exhibit. There are lots of different personality tests that one can undertake but the one we are going to concentrate on is the personality type A, B, C and D.

In these personality types, anyone can be grouped into the four categories, however, they are not exclusively grouped into just one category or type. That is because everyone will exhibit more dominant personality traits from one of the types but have elements from another.

These personality types can be used to understand a job candidate's personality among other things. From identifying people who are more likely to be a better team player, to those with characteristics set to lead, hiring managers can use these personality tests to create a team which has a more balanced environment and even improve staff retention.

As discussed, the tests are indicators into personality type, and cannot put you firmly in one category or another. There will be more dominant traits in each category type but it is rare to find people who just fit the mould of one.

We will now take a closer look at the different personality types and highlight some of the more key attributes to each letter.

Type A personality

The Type A personality is the "go getter" type. They have very high standards, are extremely competitive, love to set goals and they love to achieve as many as possible.

However, the type A personality will struggle not so much when things are going wrong, but when things are going right. Even if the outcome is positive or very good, they want to do it again because they think it can be done better.

The Type A personality can also be known as, Director.

Goal orientated, risk taker and good under stress the Type A personality will show themselves to be incredibly diligent and hardworking employees and leaders. Sometimes, too hard working with workaholic tendencies, staying as long as possible to make sure the job gets done to the exacting standards they hold. Better left working alone rather than in teams, being restricted will have significant adverse effects.

You will see many Type A personalities in senior leadership positions - or trying to get there - and even in entrepreneurship roles.

Type B personality

The Type B personality is the laid back one. These are people who are generally very grounded and peaceful in their demeanour.

Don't however think that this is someone who is very placid. On the contrary, they love being around people and love being the centre of attention. Their driving need is to be liked by pretty much everyone. Being applauded or acknowledged is key to their personality.

The Type B personality can also be known as, Socialiser.

Relationship orientated, outgoing and enthusiastic, the Type B personality will be someone who loves to talk about themselves - not to show off - but to be liked. Being well turned out and knowledgeable about many things is a driving factor for them. Any form of public humiliation is, however, devastating as it is seen as an attack on the whole person, rather than just the isolated situation.

At work, they would be the relationship builders, the ones who could cultivate better working environments with different personalities and are very good at turning ideas into workable solutions.

Type C personality

The Type C personality is the detailed one. They thrive in environments where their things are controlled and stable.

Being accurate, rational and applying logic to everything they do is where this personality really shows itself. Demanding logic over emotion is a natural dominant feature. Not suffering from hype or drama, in fact, they dislike it because they want facts and data.

The Type C personality can also be known as the Thinker.

Detail orientated, logical and prepared, this careful, resourceful and thinking personality is very good in a situation where everything needs to be analysed before any stands are taken. They like to control everything, even others which can be a negative aspect of this personality. Having all the facts at hand makes them a very difficult person to break down in opposing ideas or questioning as they interpret everything with the information they have and are given.

In a working environment, they are meticulous with the information and the data that they have to hand. You will commonly see Type C personalities in roles within science, medicine and law.

Type D personality

The Type D personality is the existentialist one. They are calm on the surface and enjoy things to remain the same as long as possible.

Hard working in nature, they are people pleasers like Type B but want to know that they are needed for their work rather than being validated over just who they are. They require a sense of security and believe that taking risks or change is actually quite dangerous and imposing on life balance.

The Type D personality can also be known as the Supporter.

Task orientated, stabilising and cautious, this very organised personality is someone who is seen as a supporter within a business. A supporter in the sense of helping others, showing compassion, thoughtfulness and caring. They need to feel part of a team, but in that team they can act as a paternal figure, helping others to achieve and never giving up on the task or the business.

In a working environment they are very good at delivering repetitive tasks - in fact, they enjoy that lack of variety because change can cause distress. They are also very good with attention to detail, making them a desirable candidate who requires stability in their role.

The most effective method to test for the 4 character types

A workplace personality test is a basic appraisal that utilizes generally acknowledged mental speculations to assist with acquiring a far-reaching understanding into an individual's reasonableness to a job. This will take a gander at things, for example, receptiveness to change, how they manage pressure, how aggressive they may be and so on.

By giving the business an elevated degree of definite knowledge on their representatives, they will actually want to recognize who falls into every one of the character types. There are likenesses and shared attributes across the four character types, just with the extra knowledge from a character test will it become clear which clients fall into each kind.

Thomas gives an extensive personality test to estimate individual characteristics and how they connect with the work environment.

How Thomas appraisals measure work environment character

Thomas' working environment personality test can be utilized to help evaluate and comprehend an applicants or representative'spersonality test and more extensive character.

In light of the around the world perceived and regarded 'Enormous 5' mental hypothesis, the High Potential Trait Indicator (or HPTI) as we additionally call it, evaluates six center attributes (Conscientiousness, Adjustment, Curiosity, Risk Approach, Ambiguity Acceptance and Competitiveness) to assist you with distinguishing the best possibility for a job and recognize authority potential, adding certainty to your enrollment.

Whether you are Type An or Type C, it is feasible to comprehend that we as a whole have various approaches to connecting with our current circumstance and individuals that we work with. We are every one of the a combination of various character types however with additional predominant aspects from one over the other. Having a grip of the more predominant aspects prompts a superior comprehension of the sort of individuals we work with and the sort of individuals we are.

Conclusion:

Personality is the collection of characteristic thoughts, feelings, and behaviors that make up a person. Human personality is a complex area of study. Not only is human nature complex, but also each individual has a unique combination of inherent abilities and preferences and learned responses. Beyond that, any researchers of personality also have certain personalities, which requires them to "bare their soul" in order to understand themselves and others.

57

CHAPTER EIGHT

Personality Nature And Trait Theories

Personality Concept

Personality refers to a person's mental and physical well-being.

personality, a characteristic way of thinking, feeling, and acting. personality embraces temperaments, perspectives, and sentiments and is most obviously communicated in connections with others. It incorporates conduct attributes, both intrinsic and obtained, that recognize one individual from one more and that can be seen in individuals' relations to the climate and to the gathering.

The term personality has been characterized in numerous ways, yet as a mental idea two principal implications have developed.

The first relates to the steady distinctions that exist between individuals: in this sense, the investigation of character centers around arranging and making sense of somewhat stable human mental attributes.

The subsequent significance stresses those characteristics that make all individuals the same and that recognize mental man from different species; it guides the character scholar to look for those consistencies among all individuals that characterize the idea of man as well as the elements that impact the course of lives. This duality might assist with making sense of the two bearings that personality studies have taken: from one viewpoint, the investigation of perpetually unambiguous characteristics in individuals, and, on the other, the quest for the coordinated entirety of mental capacities that accentuates the interchange among natural and mental occasions inside individuals and those social and organic occasions that encompass them. The double meaning of personality is interlaced in a large portion of the themes examined beneath. It ought to be accentuated, notwithstanding, that no meaning of personality has tracked down widespread acknowledgment inside the field.

Davidson writes on temperament, that is socially developed once having a genetic base, through time in his medical textbook, "Principles and observe of drugs." once passing through a succession of biological process stages, the individual reaches associate adult psychological stage.

"**Personality** is that the most applicable conceptualisation of a person's behaviour with all its characteristics, that the soul will offer in an exceedingly moment," McClelland says.

According to Davidson's conception, there area unit three completely different parts of one's temperament and its development and growth: social, physiological, and psychological. McClelland has targeted on the psychological factors that influence desired changes in {an individual's|a person's|a temperament's|a human|somebody's} behaviour and personality.

As a result, each of those ideas shed some light-weight on the formation of temperament and individual behaviour. excluding Allport's comprehensive approach to the topic, each of those definitions have the foremost application and utility in organisational behaviour.

An individual's temperament is exclusive, personal, and a primary issue of his behaviour.

Individuals answer completely different events in several ways that thanks to variances in temperament. Some temperament theorists highlight the necessity of recognising the person-situation interaction, i.e., personality's social learning parts. The study of human behaviour would profit greatly from such associate interpretation.

The four character types include:

- **Normal:** The most well-known type are individuals who are high in neuroticism and extraversion while lower in receptiveness.
- **Reserved:** People in this sort are not open or hypochondriac however they are sincerely steady. They will generally be thoughtful, pleasant and honest.
- **Role-models:** These individuals are normal pioneers with low degrees of neuroticism and elevated degrees of pleasantness, extraversion, transparency and uprightness. They pay attention to novel thoughts and are dependable.

- **Self-centered:** While these individuals score high in extraversion they rank sub optimal transparency, suitability and uprightness.

"The way for you to develop is to be familiar with yourself," Amaral said.

Personality Nature

Every person's temperament is expounded to his or her nature. In general, someone asserts himself by his temperament traits. With their years of expertise, mature folks adopt associate objective perspective toward themselves et al.. They conjointly mirror on themselves so as to reinforce their temperament and behavior.

i. Self-Consciousness:

People at large and alternative species area unit immensely completely different. His temperament is marked by a attribute notable as'self-consciousness,' that permits him to remember of his surroundings and self-identity.

ii. Atmosphere Adaptability:

Off and on, temperament will build diversifications in response to desired changes. The term "resistance to change" refers to a disagreement defined by tension and conflict. folks sometimes comply with new surroundings and obstacles. Adaptation to new settings is usually in the middle of a modification in behaviour pattern, leading to a sleek operating condition and a nice atmosphere.

iii. Goal-oriented:

Folks try and accomplish their objectives. people do have the motivation to realize their objectives. Motive is that the results of needs and necessities. a person's want leads his or her behaviour toward achieving that want. activity changes area unit influenced by each physiological and social factors.

iv. Temperament Integration:

temperament works in an exceedingly consistent manner by combining varied activities (both mental and private experiences). temperament comes in an exceedingly kind of shapes and sizes. temperament is differentiated by the style within which it's integrated. folks with developed personalities have a powerful association to their values and experiences. this can be determined by their activity standards, that they need developed from childhood.

Personality characteristics

You'll be asked to list your personal attributes if you apply for employment. Employers assume that your temperament is very fastened and will not vary considerably from year to year. whereas most folks will relate to the current notion, wherever will our temperament originate? Is it in our polymer, or is it additional a results of our formative circumstances?

The answer is, of course, both. as a result of our brain and therefore the chemicals that act inside it area unit generated by genes, there area unit bound to be genes that influence our behaviour. Finding anybody of the many genes concerned, on the opposite hand, is notoriously tough. as a result of personalities area unit complicated, the biology of behaviour is as complicated.

Scientists area unit solely currently commencing to gain a more robust understanding of however genes have an effect on behaviour.

i. Temperament is well-structured and consistent.

ii. Temperament may be a psychological attribute that's influenced by biological processes and necessities.

iii. Temperament influences however folks behave.

iv. Temperament is expressed in an exceedingly kind of ways that, together with thoughts, feelings, and behaviours.

Who Were the Neo-Freudians?

Many of the most tenets of Freud's psychotherapy theory were given by Neo-Freudian psychologists, however they updated and tailored the approach to accommodate their own beliefs, thoughts, and opinions. scientist brain doctor instructed a spread of polemic views, however he conjointly noninheritable an oversized following.

Many of those students united with Freud's ideas regarding the unconscious and therefore the importance of childhood development. alternative students, on the opposite hand, disagreed or outright rejected variety of things. As a result, these people developed their own distinct conceptions of temperament and psychological feature.

Neo-Freudian Disagreements

These neo-Freudian thinkers disagreed with neurologist for a spread of reasons. Erik Erikson, as an example, argued that brain doctor was mistaken in basic cognitive process that childhood events affected temperament virtually entirely. alternative considerations that role player neo-Freudian philosophers' attention were:

The importance of sexual needs as a basic motive in Freud's theory

The absence of social and cultural influences on behaviour and temperament in Freud's work

Sigmund Freud's demoralised read on attribute

Many neo-Freudians believed that Freud's theories were too targeted on psychopathology, sex, and childhood events.

Instead, several of them selected to focus their theories on a lot of positive aspects of attribute moreover because the social influences that contribute to temperament and behavior.1

While the neo-Freudians might are influenced by Freud, they developed their own distinctive theories and views on human development, temperament, and behavior.

Major Neo-Freudian Thinkers

There were variety of neo-Freudian thinkers World Health Organization stone-broke with the brain doctor psychotherapy tradition to develop their own psychodynamic theories. a number of these people were at first a part of Freud's set, as well as Carl Jung and male monarch Adler.

Carl Jung

Carl Jung and Freud once had an in depth relationship, however Carl Gustav Jung stone-broke away to make his own concepts.2 Carl Gustav Jung observed his theory of temperament as analytical scientific discipline, and he introduced the conception of the collective unconscious. He delineated this as a universal structure shared by all members of an equivalent species containing all of the instincts and archetypes that influence human behavior.

Jung still placed nice stress on the unconscious, however his theory placed a better stress on his conception of the collective unconscious instead of the private unconscious. Like several of the opposite neo-Freudians, Carl Gustav Jung conjointly centered less on sex than Freud did in his work.

Alfred Adler

Alfred Adler believed that Freud's theories centered too heavily on sex because the primary incentive for human behavior.3 Instead, Adler placed a lesser stress on the role of the unconscious and a larger target social and social influences.

His approach, called individual scientific discipline, was focused on the drive that each one folks need to complete their feelings of inferiority. The complex, he urged, was somebody's feelings and doubts that they are doing not qualify to people or to society's expectations.4

Erik Erikson

While Freud believed that temperament was largely set in stone throughout time of life, Erikson felt that development continuing throughout life. He conjointly believed that not all conflicts were unconscious. He thought several were aware and resulted from the method|biological process} process itself.

Erikson de-emphasized the role of sex as a incentive for behavior and instead placed a far stronger target the role of social relationships.

His eight-stage theory of psychosocial development concentrates on a series of biological process conflicts that occur throughout the period of time, from birth till death. At every stage, folks face a crisis that has got to be resolved to develop sure psychological strengths.5

Karen Horney

Karen Horney was one amongst the primary girls trained in psychotherapy, and she or he was conjointly one amongst the primary to criticize Freud's depictions of ladies as inferior to men. Horney objected to Freud's portrayal of ladies as full of "penis envy."

Instead, she steered that men expertise "womb envy" as a result of they're unable involved youngsters. Her theory focuses on however behavior was influenced by variety of various neurotic desires.

Trait Theories of Personalities

Trait theorists believe temperament are often understood by positing that every one individuals have sure traits, or characteristic ways in which of behaving. does one tend to be sociable or shy? Passive or aggressive? Optimistic or pessimistic? in keeping with the Diagnostic and applied mathematics Manual (DSM) of the yank medicine Association, temperament traits ar outstanding aspects of temperament that ar exhibited in an exceedingly wide selection of necessary social and private contexts. In alternative words, people have sure characteristics that partially confirm their behavior; these traits ar trends in behavior or angle that tend to be gift in spite of matters.

An example of a attribute is extraversion–introversion. sociableness tends to be manifested in outgoing, talkative, energetic behavior, whereas introversion is manifested in additional reserved and solitary behavior. a personal might fall on any purpose within the time, and therefore the location wherever the individual falls can confirm however he or she responds to varied things.

The idea of categorizing individuals by traits are often derived back as so much as Hippocrates; but additional fashionable theories have come back from Gordon Allport, Raymond Cattell, and Hans Eysenck.

Gordon Allport (1897–1967)

Gordon Allport was one amongst the primary fashionable attribute theorists. Allport and Henry Odbert worked through 2 of the foremost comprehensive dictionaries of English language on the market and extracted around eighteen,000 personality-describing words. From this list they reduced the amount of words to roughly four,500 temperament-describing adjectives that they thought of to explain noticeable and comparatively permanent personality traits.

Allport organized these traits into a hierarchy of 3 levels:

Cardinal traits dominate Associate in Nursingd form an individual's behavior, like Ebenezer Scrooge's greed or Mother Theresa's unselfishness. They stand at the highest of the hierarchy and ar jointly referred to as the individual's master management. they're thought of to be Associate in Nursing individual's ruling passions. Cardinal traits ar powerful, however few individuals have personalities dominated by one attribute. Instead, our personalities ar generally composed of multiple traits.

Central traits come back next within the hierarchy. These ar general characteristics found in variable degrees in all and sundry (such as loyalty, kindness, agreeableness, friendliness, sneakiness, wildness, or grouchiness). they're the essential building blocks that form most of our behavior.

Secondary traits exist at all-time low of the hierarchy and don't seem to be quite as obvious or consistent as central traits. {they ar|they're} plentiful however are solely gift below specific circumstances; they embody things like preferences and attitudes. These secondary traits justify why someone might sometimes exhibit behaviors that appear incongruent with their usual behaviors. as an example, a friendly person gets Associate in Nursinggry once individuals attempt to tickle him; another isn't an anxious person however continuously feels nervous speaking in public.

Allport hypothesized that internal Associate in Nursingd external forces influence an individual's behavior and temperament, and he stated these forces as genotypes and phenotypes. Genotypes ar internal forces that relate to however someone retains data and uses it to act with the globe. Phenotypes ar external forces that relate to the approach a personal accepts his or her surroundings and the way others influence his or her behavior.

Raymond Cattell (1905–1998)

In a trial to create Allport's list of four,500 traits additional manageable, Raymond Cattell took the list and removed all the synonyms, reducing the amount right down to 171. However, speech communication that a attribute is either gift or absent doesn't accurately replicate a person's individuation, as a result of (according to attribute theorists) all of our personalities are literally created from constant attributes; we have a tendency to take issue solely within the degree to that every trait is expressed.

Cattell believed it necessary to sample a large vary of variables to capture a full understanding of temperament. the primary kind of knowledge was life knowledge, that involves aggregation data from Associate in Nursing individual's natural existence behaviors. Experimental knowledge involves activity reactions to standardized experimental things, and form knowledge involves gathering responses supported thoughtfulness by a personal concerning his or her own behavior and feelings. exploitation this knowledge, Cattell performed correlational analysis to generated sixteen dimensions of human temperament traits: preoccupancy, warmth, apprehension, emotional stability, liveliness, openness to alter, disposition, privateness, intelligence , rule consciousness , tension, sensitivity, social boldness, independence, vigilance, and dominance.

Based on these sixteen factors, he developed a questionnaire referred to as the 16PF. rather than a attribute being gift or absent, every dimension is scored over a time, from high to low. as an example, your level heatth|of heat} describes however warm, caring, and nice to others you're. If you score low on this index, you tend to be additional distant and cold. A high score on this index signifies you're corroboratory and comforting. Despite reducing considerably on Allport's list of traits, Cattell's 16PF theory has still been criticized for being too broad.

Hans Eysenck (1916–1997)

Hans Eysenck was a temperament theorizer World Health Organization targeted on temperament—innate, genetically primarily based temperament variations. He believed temperament is essentially ruled by biology, and he viewed individuals as having 2 specific temperament dimensions: sociableness vs. introversion and psychological disorder vs. stability. once collaborating together with his married woman and fellow temperament theorizer Sybil H. J. Eysenck, he supplementary a 3rd dimension to the present model: psychoticism vs. socialization.

According to their theory, individuals high on the attribute of sociableness area unit sociable and outgoing and without delay connect with others, whereas individuals high on the attribute of introversion have the next have to be compelled to be alone, interact in solitary behaviors, and limit their interactions with others.

In the neuroticism/stability dimension, individuals high on psychological disorder tend to be associate degreexious; they have a tendency to possess an active sympathetic systema nervosum and even with low stress, their bodies and spirit tend to travel into a flight-or-fight reaction. In distinction, individuals high on stability tend to want additional stimulation to activate their flight-or-fight reaction and area unit so thought-about additional showing emotion stable.

Conclusion

The study of the theories of temperament is vital for college students because it prompts the requirement tounderstand why individuals behave as they are doing. Also, this space of study enlightens individuals on the requirement to be a lot of kind once judgement others supported however they behave since it's going to not be as a results of their own selection. The theories of privateity ar numerous relating to the character of personal behavior descriptions. additionally to the common theories, a reasonably uncommon conception, epigenetics is highlighted within the study of temperament theories. the range of personalities and therefore the relationships between the theories describing them points to the very fact that the human observation done by the theorists was correct to an oversized extent.

CHAPTER NINE

PERSONALITY AND ASSESSMENT OF PERSONALITY

Introduction

The term personality is derived from the Latin word 'Persona' which means the mask worn by the Roman actors. It implies that personality refers to the individual as seen by others. When the layman speaks of 'personality' he is generally referring to the overall impression one person makes on another.

The definitions of personality that are mostly widely used by psychologists may be grouped into four classes or categories:

i.   omnibus definitions
ii. integrative definitions
iii. totality definitions and
iv. definitions that emphasize adjustment.

Omnibus definitions take into account all of the processes or activities of which the individual is capable- such as interests, habits and abilities. In general, however, neglect the integrative aspects of personality. Integrative definitions emphasize the organization of personality. e.g., personality is the integrated organization of all the cognitive, conative, affective and physical characteristics of an individual as it manifests itself in focal distinctness from others. (Warren 1934). Totality definitions emphasizes the integration or pattern of the various aspects that make up personality but tend to obscure the component parts and adjustment definitions tend to emphasize the individual's characteristic pattern of adjustments.

'Personality is unique organization of characteristics that determines the individual's typical or recurrent pattern of behaviour.' This definition has several ideas concerning personality that are generally accepted by psychologists. First, there is the idea that personality is unique. Second, personality is viewed as being composed of many characteristics in a particular organization. Finally, the unique organization of characteristics is seen as determining a typical or consistent pattern of behaviour.

Assessment Of Personality

Assessment is a wider term than measurement. Measurement denotes quantity and assessment denotes quality. Assessment of personality is a comprehensive task because personality cannot be assessed using a single check-list, an isolated anecdotal record or a battery of tests. A complete assessment will require the use of several techniques.

Various problems are faced in the assessment of personality. Since long psychologists have been trying to evolve robustprocedures for assessing personality yet even today, they are far away from the goal. There are three basic reasons for not arriving at exact conclusions-

- complex nature of the individual whose personality is to be assessed,
- complex nature of the person who assesses the personality and
- nature of assessment instrument.

Assessment of personality does not remain stable because an individual is ever growing and he may not respond to the same situation in the same way. There are various intrinsic and extrinsic factors which control him constantly. Moreover, an individual being assessed is capable of employing hundred ways to evade being assessed. Even if he cooperates, he may not be in a position to understand and express himself about his unconscious mind. Thus, we may peep into a person's personality here and there but a total study of personality eludes us.

Subjectivity of the person who assesses can also influence assessment. Even when the same person assessed the same individual and different intervals under the same conditions, result may differ.

In psychological measurement, we do not have any regular unit of measurement. In personality assessment there is no zero point for reference. Thus, exact measurement is not possible. Above all, tools of personality assessment are not very definite, stable and accurate in terms of their outcomes. However, numerous methods of assessing personality have been developed. Even by using these methods we get only an estimate of personality since personality is dynamic and its correct measurement is not possible. A few methods of assessing personality are as follows:

Method of autobiography:

Using cue words, a person is asked to write about himself. He is expected to report from memory so that one can get a picture of his personality. But there is every possibility that the person has forgotten relevant information. Also, he might imagine and report about things in a subjective manner. Hence this method has limited reliability.

Questionnaire or inventory method:

This consists of a standard set of questions about aspects of the individual's life history, feeling, preferences or activities, presented in a standard way and scored with a standard scoring key. Unlike observational methods which give us an understanding of only overt behaviour, inventories help us assess not noy the overt but also the covert manifestation of personality. Inner characteristics such as how the person feels about himself, feelings of self-confidence etc. are measured. There are several different types of personality inventories. These include-

- those which assess specified traits like dominance, conservatism etc.
- those which evaluate adjustment to several aspects of environment like school, community etc.
- those which classify into clinical groups and
- those which evaluate interests, values etc.

Examples of such inventories are Woodworth's Data Sheet, California Psychological Inventory, Minnesota Multiphasic Personality Inventory, Edward's Preference Schedule etc. Responding to inventories is easy since the individual has only to indicate yes/no or place a tick mark. The method is cheap and useful but there is every possibility of fake response.

Interview method:

In this method, competent psychologists place questions before the interviewee and try to elicit information which will be useful in understanding his personality. Besides the responses given by the individual, the mood and facial expressions are also studied.

Observational method:

This method is used to assess personality from the point of view of overt manifestation. Rating scales and interviews are classified as observational methods. Checklist is also one such device. Various attributes of personality are listed and the candidate/subject is rated on these. Rating may be carried out by one person or a few persons who are known to the subject. In this, it is important that the subject is intimately well known to the rater so that the rating is done correctly. In order to increase objectivity, many raters could be employed to rate a single subject.

Anecdotal records:

These are running descriptions of actual examples of behaviour of a student as observed by teachers and counsellor. It is followed by comments. Generally anecdotal records are maintained in respect of students. According to Brown and Martin, 'Anecdotes are descriptive accounts of episodes or occurrences in the daily life of a student.' An anecdotal record is a simple statement of an incident deemed by the observer to be significant with respect to a given pupil. There is no limit to the number of anecdotes that can be recorded. These provide specific and exact description of personality and minimize generalizations.

Case study method:

The record of case history of a person contains detailed information about every aspect of the individual including his heredity, incidents in his life, successes and failures, his environment etc. On the basis of all this information a detailed study of his personality is made. Allport states, "Successful case study is seen naturally to fall into three categories: a) a description of the person's status, b) an account of past influences and successive stages of development and c) a manifestation of future tendency."

Situational tests of personality:

In this method certain situations are created and the individual is observed in these situations. The reactions of the individual are carefully studied and personality is measured. The main defect of this method is that the situation is artificial and the response we get may not be the real response which the individual would give in the actual situation.

Sociometric method:

One aspect about personality is the extent to which an individual socializes with others in a group situation. Sociometry was designed by J.L.Moreno and Helen Jennings in 1946. According to them, sociometry may be described as a means of presenting simply and graphically the entire structure of relations existing at a given time among members of a given group. The major lines of communication or the pattern of attraction and repulsion in its full scope are made readily comprehensive at a glance. Being peer rating rather than rating by supervisors, sociometry adds another valid dimension of understanding the personality of an individual. The relationship among group members is depicted by sociogram.

Projective techniques:

These measure the global or overall character of personality, in contrast with the atomistic or trait approach of inventories. Besides, since such techniques involve the use of unstructured stimulus materials their purpose is disguised. Thus, unlike the personality inventory which may be consciously or unconsciously falsified by the subject, such falsification is generally extremely difficult on any of the projective techniques. Most projective techniques involve the presentation of unstructured stimuli- ink blots, incomplete sentences, incomplete stories and so on. In each case, the subject structures or organizes the stimuli through the projection of his own personality. It is a well-known fact that internal factors have an important role in perception- attitudes, values, motives are maximized when the individual is faced with an unstructured stimulus. Hence, when we show an individual an ambiguous stimulus such as ink blots and ask what he perceives, his responses are primarily determined by his characteristics as a perceiver. In the projective techniques, the subject's perception provides us with an approach to studying personality.

The most widely used projective technique is the **Rorschach** developed by Swiss Psychologist, Herman Rorschach in 1921. It consists of ten ink blots. Five of the blots are different in shades of black or grey, while the other five are in various colors.

The blots are presented to the subject one at a time and always in the same order. With each one, the subject is asked to tell what the blot resembles or what he sees. Responses are written down and the subject is allowed to look at each card as long as he likes. He may also turn the card in any direction.

After the subject has looked at all the ten cards, the examiner then conducts an inquiry to ascertain the specific part of the blot to which the subject was responding and also to determine the characteristics of the blot- color, shading, form- that made the subject give specific responses. Scoring of the protocol- the record of responses is made on the basis of information gained in the inquiry.

Each response on the Rorschach is scored in several ways- location, determinants, content, popularity and organization. Scoring of Rorschach is complicated and requires intensive training. Interpretation is even more complicated. It is based partially on the number of responses scored in a particular way, relative to the total number of responses. e.g., responses to color are believed to be related to emotionality or the affective characteristics of personality. Hence, if what that individual perceives is determined primarily by the color of the blot and accordingly by its shape or form and there are relatively large number of such responses- it is assumed that the person is highly emotional. His behaviour is likely to be determined mainly by his feelings and only secondarily by his intellect. Among other determinants of responses perceived on the Rorschach are human movement assumed to reflect fantasy activity, shading believed to reflect depression.

There is no cook book technique for interpreting the Rorschach. In other words, the examiner cannot look in a manual for an interpretation of a specific proportion of color responses, the meaning of specific content response, or the exact IQ level of a particular organization score.The overall interpretation of the record is dependent upon the training and experience of the examiner, his familiarity with the types of responses given by those with certain personality characteristics and the particular theory of personality to which he ascribes.

The **Thematic Apperception Test(TAT)**consists of 19 cards containing ambiguous pictures and one blank card. The subject is instructed to make up a story in connection with each of the pictures- to describe what is going on, how the people in the story feel, what led up to the incident in the picture and how it will turn out. In connection with the blank card, he is instructed to imagine a picture and make up a story to go along with it.

Morgan and Murray who developed the tests in 1935 suggest that the test be administered through two, one-hour sessions with 10 cards used in each session. However, many psychologists do not adhere to this method of administration. They simply select those pictures which they believe will elicit the most valuable information about the subject's personality. Unlike the Rorschach there is no complex scoring system generally used for the TAT. Instead, the examiner looks for 'themes' reflected in the subject's stories that may reveal something of his motives and conflicts. In this connection, it is assumed that the subjects identify with one of the characters in each picture and hence the feelings described are believed to be those of subject himself.

Often the TAT is used in conjunction with the Rorschach. Some theorists believe that the primary value of the Rorschach is in providing as assessment of the structure or make up of personality. The primary value of the TAT is assumed to rest in its reflection of the content of personality.

Other projective techniques are Blacky Test, Draw-a-Man test etc. While the advantage of the Projective techniques include its global assessment and avoidance of falsity, the main disadvantage is the scoring and interpretation since it allows for a great degree of subjectivity of the examiner to come to play. Projective techniques are all inadequately standardized, since they are validated through a procedure known as blind matching of protocol with case history. Validation is deficient in this case. However, the techniques provide valuable leads which can be followed up by psychotherapy. If these tests are better standardized that may prove to be valuable techniques for assessing personality.

CHAPTER TEN

FREUD'S PSYCHOANALYTIC THEORY ON PERSONALITY: FEMINIST APPROACHES ON GENDER CONSTRUCTION

Introduction

Freud's psychoanalytic theory, personality develops in stages, each of which is characterized by a certain degree of internal mental conflict. Sigmund Freud ' s psychoanalytic theory of personality argues that human behavior is the result of the interaction of the three parts of the mind: the id, ego and super-ego. This theory is known as Freud's structural theory of personality, which is strongly focused on the role of unconscious psychological conflicts in shaping behavior and personality. The dynamic interactions between the key components of the mind are thought to develop through the use of five different psychosexual stages of development. However, in the last century, Freud's ideas have been the subject of criticism, in part because of his emphasis on sexuality as the most important driver of the development of one's personality. According to Freud, our personality develops as a result of interaction between what is offered in the three most important structures of the human mind: the id, ego and super-ego. The conflict between these three structures, and we strive to have a balance between all of those "desires" to determine how we are to conduct ourselves and how we relate to the world. How do we achieve balance in a given situation, determine how to resolve the conflict between the two different behavioral tendencies; our biological aggressive and pleasure-seeking drives vs. our socialized internal control over those drives.

The Id

The Id is the most primitive of the three structures, is concerned with instant gratification of basic physical needs, and motivations. It works in a completely unconscious (without consciously having to think). For example, if you're *ID* walked past by a stranger consuming ice cream, then, most likely, to have this for itself. It doesn't know, or care, that it would be impolite to accept something that someone else; you are only interested in having that ice cream.

Super-ego

Super-ego is in related to the social principles and moral values which is similar to what a lot of people say it is known as "moral compass". It develops as the child learns what is good and what is bad in the part of their culture. If you're super-ego is passed through the same, or a stranger, he should take out for ice cream, because you knew that it would be rude. However, if you have the id and super-ego are involved, and id be strong enough to overcome your super-ego's fears, on the ice, but after that, you would most likely feel guilty and ashamed for your actions.

The Ego

In distinction to the instinctual id and the moral superego, and the ego is the rational, pragmatic part of our personality. It is less primitive than the id and is partly conscious and partly unconscious. This is what Freud believed that the self and the goal are to balance the demands of the id and the super-ego, in the practical context of the real thing. So, if you walked past the stranger with ice-cream, and your ego is to mediate the conflict between the id (I want to have that ice cream cone now) and the superego (It is wrong to take other people's ice cream), and you decided to buy their own. While this may mean that you will have to wait another 10 minutes, which will hinder your id, your ego, and superego decides to make that sacrifice, as part of a compromise to satisfy his desire for ice cream, or avoidance of an unpleasant social situation, and the potential embarrassment. Freud believed that the id, ego, and superego are in constant conflict, and that adult personality and behavior has its roots in the outcome of this internal conflict during childhood. He believed that a person who has a strong ego, a person, a sound, and a disturbance in the system can lead to neurosis (what we now call anxiety and depression, and unhealthy behaviors.

Psychosexual stages of development

Freud believed that the nature of the conflict between the id, ego and super-ego, changes over time, if a person is changing from a child to an adult. In particular, he argues that such conflicts have to go through a series of stages, each with a different sexual orientation: oral, anal, phallic, latent, and genital. He referred to the idea that the psychosexual theory of development, in which each of the psychosexual stage, which is directly related to the physical center of the fun. Freud's theory of psychosexual development comprises five stages. According to Freud, each stage is carried out in a period of your life. If a person is preoccupied in each of the four stages, he or she develops a personality, according to a certain stage, and the focus. The first stage, the oral stage. The baby at this stage is from birth to eighteen months. The oral phase is focused on the pursuit of pleasure, from the mouth of the baby. At this stage the need for the testing and the related vacuum, visible to the fun. Oral stimulation and it is of paramount importance at this stage as to meet the needs of the child are not met during this time period; the focus will be on the oral stage. A fixation at this stage can result in an adult's habits, such as thumb sucking, smoking, eating too much, and a nail-biting. At your age, personal characteristics, are associated with the oral fixation may also occur; these characteristics are optimism, and independence, or pessimism and hostility. The second stage is the anal stage, which lasts from eighteen months to three years. At this stage, the child's pleasure-seeking centres are located in the intestines and bladder. During this period, the parents are to pay special attention to the potty training and bowel control. The fixation at the anal stage might lead to anal-retentive. Anal retentive characteristics include excessive conscientiousness, accuracy, and good order, while the anal ban is going to disorganization, disorder, and destruction. The third stage is the phallic stage. It begins at the age of three years old, and lasts for up to six. Now the sensitivity is focused on the genitals, masturbation (for both sexes) is a new source of pleasure. The child will begin to understand the anatomical differences between men and women, which have led to a sense of jealousy and fear, which Freud called the Oedipus complex (in boys). Later, the Freudian scholars are added to the Electra complex (in girls). The fourth stage is that of the secret place, starting at the age of six, and it will run until the end, but maybe not. At this stage, not a single part of your body and looking to have fun instead of all of the sexual feelings are repressed. In this way, children can develop social skills, and comfort in social interactions with peers and family members. In the final stage of psychosexual development is the genital stage. This stage begins at the age of eleven, and continues up to the age of puberty, and ends when a person reaches adulthood at the age of eighteen years of age. The onset of puberty, which reflects a person's strong interest in a person to other opposite sexes. If a person does not have experience with the consent of the psychosexual stages, the reach of the genital stage, they will have a well-balanced person.

Criticism of Freud's theory

Even though Freud's theories have a number of advantages that have contributed to the expansion of our psychological understanding of personality, and they are not open-ended. The focus is on the structure of human consciousness, Freud's little attention has been paid to the influence of the environment, the social sciences or the world. His theories were strongly committed to the region, and to a large extent ignored the "normal" healthy effect. He has also been criticized for his narrow minded attitude to human sexuality, to the exclusion of other important factors. Many critics point out that Freud's theories are not supported by the empirical (experimental) evidence. In fact, when scientists began to examine his ideas of a more scientifically, it has become clear that some of them could not be confirmed that a theory is scientific, it needs to be able to rule out ("forge"), as well as the experimental evidence, and many of Freud's ideas are not falsifiable. It is worth pointing out, and contemporary critics have been very critical of many of Freud's theories, which seems to indicate that the accounting policies and methods of psychoanalytic theory, is deeply patriarchal (male-dominated), and anti-feminist, and misogynistic (anti-women). Karen Horney, a psychologist, traveled to Freud, they believed that the "Freudian approach as a foundation, "the male one." Feminist Betty Friedan referred to Freud's concept of penis envy" is purely a social bias that is typical of the Victorian era, and demonstrates how this concept played a crucial role in discrediting alternative ideas regarding the female in the beginning and in the middle of the twenty-first century.

Neo-Freudian approaches to personality

Even though Sigmund Freud was an important contribution to the field of psychology, it is thanks to his psychoanalytic theory of personality; his work was not well studied. Many people have made criticisms of his theories, the focus is on issues of sexuality; and, in the years that have passed, it is his work, and many, many other researchers have tweaked and developed his ideas for the creation of a new theory of the personality. This is the neo-Freudian theorists generally agreed with Freud that childhood experiences were important, but they have reduced the emphasis on sex and sexuality. Instead of a strictly biological approach to the development of personality, such as Freud did, by focusing on the individual, the evolutionary gestures), they focus more holistically on how the social context and culture impact on the individual's development. A lot of psychologists, scientists, and philosophers have made significant additions to the psychoanalytic studies of the personality. The four most well-known neo-Freudians include Alfred Adler, Erik Erikson, Carl Jung and Karen Horney.

Alfred Adler

Alfred Adler was the first to explore the development of a comprehensive social, psychodynamic theory of personality. He founded a school of psychology called individual psychology, which focuses on what we need to do in order to compensate for feelings of inferiority. Adler introduced the concept of the inferiority complex, that is, how a person's feelings that they don't matter, and does not conform to the standards of others or of the community. He, too, believed in the importance of social relations, in view of the fact that the child will be considered during the development of the social development, on the site of the sexual phase, described by Freud. On the basis of these ideas, Amenities and identifies three important tasks that all of us have to solve are: occupational tasks (careers), social (friendship), and love tasks (such as finding a partner for a long-term relationship.

Eric Erickson

Erik Erikson is best-known for the proposal of the psycho-social theory of development, in which it is assumed that a person's personality develops over a lifetime, on the basis of social relationships, and a departure from Freud's biology is focused on the view. In his psychological theory, Erickson emphasized the social relationships, which is the case in each of the stages of development of the personality, in contrast to Freud, who stresses the need to have sex. Erickson has identified eight stages, each of which is a dispute or a challenge. The development of a healthy personality and a sense of competence are subject to the successful completion of each task.

Carl Jung

Carl Jung is followed by Adler's footsteps, to the development of a theory of personality, in which analytical psychology, it is concerned. One of Jung's most important contributions was the concept of the collective unconscious, which he regarded as Freud's, as the "universal" version of the personal unconscious mental patterns, or memory traces, which are common to all of us (Jung, 1928). These ancestral memories, which, Jungian archetypes, are represented by the universal themes expressed in terms of the art and literature of the different cultures, as well as the dreams of the people. Jung introduced the concept of the persona, which refers to a kind of "mask" that is what we have on the basis of our experience, and in this course, as it is in our collective unconscious. Jung believed that the person is acting as a trade-off between who we really are (our true self) and the society expect from us; we hide behind a mask, which can be the parts of ourselves that do not meet up to the expectations of the society.

Karen Horney

Karen Horney was one of the first women to be trained as a Freudian psychoanalyst. Karen Horney's theories have focused on the "unconscious anxiety", which, she believed, came from the early childhood experiences, needs and challenges, of loneliness and / or isolation. Karen theorized the three styles of coping that they take in relation to fear of movement in the direction of people, moving away from the people and for the movement of people. Karen Horney was also a major influence on the development of feminism in the field of psychodynamics. To Freud, it is often criticized for the installation of almost all men for what some see as a retreat for the women; for example, Horney disagreed with the Freudian idea that the girls are jealous of the penis, and is jealous of the men of biological functions. According to Horney, each and every blind is the most likely to the level of permissions that are often people who have it, which means that the differences between men's and women's personalities emerge from the dynamics of culture, not of biology. Furthermore, it suggests that men experience womb envy" because they don't have.

Gender-based socialization

One way to interpret that Beauvoir's declaration of a person is not born, but becomes, a woman has to take it as an indication of the socialization of gender, females become women, and the processes by which they are acquiring female characteristics, and learn how women's behavior. It is believed that masculinity and femininity is the product of the nurse or the nursing units. They may be causally structured (Haslanger, 1995), social forces have a main playing role in the development of the gender of the individuals, and (in some sense) to shape the way in which they become, women, and men. The mechanism of the activities of social learning. For example, Kate Millett, is of the opinion that the gender differences between men and women above all, the cultural rather than the biological foundation, which is the result of a variety of relationships, (Millet, 1971). For her, gender is the fullness of your parents, peers, and culture, the perception of what is appropriate for one's gender, temperament, personality, interests, status, dignity, a gesture and a word (Millett 1971). Male-and-female-gender-norms, however, are a problem in the generation of behavior that fits comfortably in the subordination of women, and to ensure that women are socialized in a subordinate role in society, they are taught to be passive, ignorant, easy-going, emotional, machines for men. However, because these roles are to be taken into account, we can create a more equal society, and "unlearning" of social roles. That is, women should aim to reduce the impact of socialization. Social learning theorists believe that there are such a lot of different influences that is to socialize us, women as well as men. In this case, it's very hard to stand up to gender socialization. For example, parents are often unaware of the treatment for male and female children differently. When parents were asked to describe it, it is available 24 hours a day for the kids, and they were, therefore, the use of gender-stereotyped language, the boys are described as strong, alert, and in a consistent manner, and the girls are described as " a small, soft, and tender. Parents ' attitudes toward their children will also give the descriptions, whether they are aware of it or not (Renzetti & Curran 1992). Some of socialization, it is even more pronounced: the children are often dressed up in a sex-stereotyped clothing and colors, the boys are dressed in blue and girls in pink, and the parents tend to buy their children's gender-stereotyped toys and games. They also have the tendency to (intentionally or not), and to strengthen some of the "good" behavior. Although the precise form of the socialization of the sexes has changed a lot since the arrival of the second wave of feminism, and even today, girls are not encouraged to play sports, such as football, or playing the "rough and tumble" of the game, and they are more likely than boys to the doll or other accessories, toys to play-the boys are told not to "cry like a baby" and give men's toys such as cars and guns. According to the theories of social learning, children will also have an impact on what we see in the world. This makes it more difficult to counter gender socialization. First of all, in the books of the children, men and women are represented in real life stereotypes, for example, men, women, and leaders, as well as the women's assistant and the students. One of the best ways to deal with gender stereotyping in children's books, and was the portrayal of women in an independent role, while the men were not aggressive, and health care (Renzetti & Curran 1992). Some publishers have attempted to use an alternative approach, which makes their characters-for example, gender neutral, animals, or asexual imaginary creatures, (such as the teletubbies on TV). However, the parents in the book, of gender-neutral or genderless characters are often undermining the publishers of the efforts made by them to read with their children in such a way that the characters are either male or female. According to Renzetti and Curran, parents are called, and the vast majority of those are gender-neutral, male characters, such as characters, that are compatible with the female gender stereotypes (such as good) and were referred to as a woman (Renzetti & Curran, 1992). The interacting effects of these are thought to have implicit messages about how men and women should behave, and it is expected that you will work through us, created in both female and male personalities.

Psychoanalytic feminism

Psychoanalytic feminism is the theory of grief, which states that men have a psychological need to submit to women. The roots of the men's desire for dominance over women, and women with the minimum of resistance, and the submission to lie deep within the human psyche. This branch of feminism that strives to gain knowledge about how the life of a reason to evolve in order to better understands it and to change it, the oppression of women. The model reduction is also integrated in the society, and the creation and maintenance of patriarchy. With the help of psychoanalytic methods in order to examine the differences between men and women, as well as ways to build the gender, you can reorganize the socialization of the models are in the early stages of the human life. Social change or "cure" may be made by the open-source of the complete dominance in the male psyche, and submission of the female psyche and that is largely unnoticed, in the ignorance of the people.

Psychoanalysis and feminism

"The Second Sex" by Simon de Beauvoir (1949), and "The Feminine Mystique" by Betty Friedan (1963), both theorized psychoanalysis as stated women as being inferior, and defined only in relation to men. Then, in the 1970s, a second wave of feminist works, such as Kate Millet's Sexual Politics (1970) The Dialectic of Sex by Shulamith Firestone (1970), and Germaine Greer's The Female Eunuch (1970), has called for changes in the society, which is helping to tackle sexual inequality. Mitchell's book, Psychoanalysis and Feminism (1972), was an important milestone in the revival of the analysis, and the interpretation of the revolutionary concept of the women. As of the start of the analysis, the argument is that the physical reality of the race is to be distinguished from the anatomical fact, that there is no clear correlation between the fields of biology and psychology. Men and women have been physically or socially "made" as men or the women, but they become such. Initially, however, as Freud assumed, a symmetry in the development of what he called the Oedipus complex. Alone, in an essay written in 1925, it was for Freud, a distinction should be made between the psychosexual history of the boys and girls, and recognizing the importance of the pre-oedipal phase, in which the boys and girls, for the love of the mother, and the two have to abandon her in favor of the father (1925). A young girl with the love of her mother, her father, and it is as if a man wants to be a mother, in the sense that, later on, his wife. In this model, the boys identify with their fathers, and because of their masculine identity are determined. A boy learns of his role as a father, the heir. The girl, on the other hand, has to be able to identify with the mother, while at the same time, a rejection of her as an object of love, the love, object and turning to her father instead.

According to Freud, the date of the rejection by the mother, it is based on the frustration, and the frustration that is not able to meet her mother's, and it goes hand in hand with the enemy. The importance of pre oedipal relationship a mother has been fully discussed, since Freud's time. Recently, interest in the nature of a female's personality is reflected in the works of Ethel Guy, Irene, Soon, and Jessica Benjamin, and in the United States, as well as in the work of Janine Chasseguet-Smirgel, Catherine J., and Jean-Parat, Marie, and Toroc, and Joyce McDougall in France. In the 1920's, a controversy broke out on the perception of femininity. If Freud's libido, it is the same for both sexes; it is, in the English language school by the female sex drive is. Karen Horney and Ernest Jones who took part in a series of exchanges, and argued against Freud's view of the making of a "positive" image of women's sexuality is distinct from the concept of the provision of services. For Jones, the evolution of the female is associated with a physical constitution. In a legal dispute with him, as well as Freud pointed out that he deeply understood the basic nature of the sexuality, and that he had been restored to the biological reductionism. Mitchell said that, in the Freud - Jones, the controversy has shifted to the question of the differences between men and women, on what is specific to each gender. The development of the psychoanalytic theory in the UK, along with the school of objects relations, and lead to a focus on the parent-child dyad and the role of motherhood. Psychoanalytic work from the early focusing on the poor conditions in the early stages, and gradually, the attention is focused on the impact of the poor conditions at the time of transfer. Melanie Klein's theory continued to Freud, the shift of emphasis from the father, the mother, and the importance of a mother to the children of both sexes. In front of her, and the relationship of the child to the mother's body has been described above, the emotional life. In particular, the breast is a ratio; it is of crucial importance in a child's early experiences. Klein's concept of the instructive, and projective identification, are metaphors for the body of the processes of the absorption of the movement. According to Klein, it's a little girl who believes that her mother's body has everything it needs, including those of her father's penis. The result of this is a girl who is full of hatred for her mother, and wants to attack you and rob you of the inside of the body. After that, she filled out due to the fear of being "having the inside of her body robbed and destroyed." In 1928, the Small, pointed out that it is in the chest, discomfort, and it is not the discovery of the lack of a penis, the girl away from her mother to her father.

Later on, she played down the child of the first one breast, jealousy, envy, and he wrote specifically about heterosexual attraction to young girls. A small view of the early mother-child relationship, and the effect of some earlier work on the subject of femininity in society, more reasonable approach is to start with the investment by the funds in advance so that you are prepared for the purpose. Progressive psychoanalysts from all sections of British society, and was inspired by the work of Klein, Donald Winnicott, Marjorie Brierly, and Wilfred Bion, which emphasizes the connection between the primary emotional development, and object relationships. These patterns can be found in the writings of Marion Burgner Pink and Adcumbe, Aigle Laufer, Dinora Pines, Said Brin, Joan Raphael-Leff, and Rosina Perelberg. In a later collection, this is found in the work of the three schools of psycho-analysis in the British Psychoanalytical Society, and Raphael-Leff, and Perelberg emphasis primal connection to the mother, and for her appearances in the transference and counter transference. American feminists believe that the analysis provides a patriarchal inequality. Nancy Chodorrow is one of the best-known writers in the United States, on the connection between psycho-analysis and feminism. The Reproduction of Mothering: Psychoanalysis and the Sociology of Gender (1978) introduced American readers to the work of the Winnicott, W. Ronald Fairbairn, and Harry Gantrip. Chodorow stresses on development in relation to the others, with a focus on the pre-Oedipal relationship between mother and child. They will have the function of being a mother to an asymmetric relationship between the boys and the girls. Girl has more permeable boundaries in your relationships with others and, as a result of the fact that she's a mother, a person of the same sex. Why do girls and women are more devoted to being a mother. The boys, on the contrary, they will develop a sense of self-esteem, in contrast to the mother, and to set more stringent limits. Men's perceptions of themselves are more spread out. Jean Baker Miller, and Carol Gilligan, of the School of inter-personal Analysis to emphasize the feminine traits of a relationship, moved to pity, and to make sure that it can be considered to be a decline in a male-dominated culture. These interpersonal theorists emphasize the cultural focus on the different characteristics of men and women, and the focus is less on the inner world of unconscious fantasies, and the internal object relations. Jessica Benjamin in the "Bond of Love" (1988) and, see both, boys, and girls looking for their father, and to confirm it. While the boy's identity is confirmed by the father, the girl in contrast has her identification with the father's power denied, and he becomes the object of her ideal ego. This will prevent her from having a "will of its own, and her desire for her father to be tinge with masochism, issues of power and submission in the sphere of relationships. Chodorow, the argument is that what all these authors have in common, despite their differences, the strain on their sites as "not applicable" (or the non-acceptance of the relationship). She argues that this position is an abrupt break with the essentialist view of gender, and is moving in the direction of the view that, by default, masculinity and femininity, in order relationally constructed context. These schools, but in the end, the building of a more stable view of femininity and masculinity than Earlier, which is, in principle, to the fact that there is a flow between masculinity and femininity in both men and women. These features can be compared with the latest trends in the French theories of psychoanalysis, and feminism, which is to emphasize unconscious fantasies, and desires, and try to find a language for the expression of the feminine principle. Below are the French psychoanalysts, in particular, there is an opinion that the "discovery" of the unconscious is, in itself, does not reveal the fact that the person is in a state of fantasy and desire. This is a radical perspective in the analysis can provide with feminism. The impact of the work of Jacques Lacan, permeates much of the work of those who accept the postulates of Freudian theory, and to those who, like Julia Kristeva, Helene Sixus, Michel Montreulet, Sarah Kofman, and Luce Irigaray continued to be very critical for the analysis of the basic assumptions. Lacan pointed out, that is, the difference between the penis and the phallus, it is fundamental to Freud's distinction between the biological and psychological reality. The phallus is the anatomical reality; it is a symbol of the mother's desire. Joel Dor suggested that the central question of the Oedipus complex, and it is, therefore, "to be or not to be the phallus," which is to say, to be or not to be to the object of her desire. The role of the father is symbolic; it represents the possibility of the object of their desire. The phallus, as opposed to penis enlargement, it is of no one (neither male nor female, and is a combination of the two genders. Chasseguet-Smirgel, McDougall, Torok, Luquet Parat, Monique Cournet-Jeannin, and Jacqueline Schaeffer have all said, from the point of view of psycho-analysis. Chasseguet-Smirgel pointed out, in her perception, the fact that the girl knew about the existence of a vagina, almost from the beginning, though, she suggests that the "know-how" that can be ruled out, the unconscious, what is the girl, well knows, and you don't know. Some of his works, "penis envy" is defined as having a protective role. For many of the French feminist writers, and the body is the locus of the female, as well as a range of work that tries to capture it in its rhythms, In her book," Speculum " (1974), Irigaray explores the psycho-analysis as an awareness of the historical and philosophical determinants of the private discourse, and the analysis of their own unconscious fantasies. In addition, being a product of a patriarchal society, it can analyze what it owes to the mother. She constantly puts herself in the position where women don't have any personal identify. She emphasizes the girl by her mother's body. The girl, says Irigaray , has the mother, in a sense, in her skin, the wetness of its mucous membrane, in the vicinity of what is most intimate to share, it is in the mystery of her posture, pregnancy, childbirth, and sexual identity. Kristeva links of spiritual suppression, the real structure of the language, and describes the pre oedipal stage, as a play of the body's rhythms, and to pre linguistic exchange between the child and the child's mother. Kristeva refers to that which Plato, in the Timaeus, called the chora as the site of the undifferentiated bodily space the mother and the child share. Inside the Oedipus complex that is dominated by the last of the unified text, or cultural knowledge. This is the difference between the semiotic and the symbolic, in retrospect, for it is only by means of a symbolic of a person to have access to the semiotic. For For Kristeva, subjectivity is founded on a constitutive repression of the maternal, the chora, the semiotic, and the abject (liminal states, like pregnancy). Kristeva has been accused of leading women, a mother's job, but it is also seen as a way in order to have a better understanding on pre oedipal.. Interestingly enough, if you go back to Freud's concept of hysteria. The occurrence of the first psychoanalytic patient, Anna O., included mutism, paralysis, "time-missing," and gaps in memory: all expressing interruptions in the domain of a reality which is being denied. Psychoanalysis indicates that sexuality is only created through division and discontinuity, although femininity is the side that both represents, and tends to be represented as, the negative (of masculinity).

Conclusion

In the analysis, is a critical diagnostic project, you do not necessarily have the legislative or policy. Due to the development of a theory of motivation, and the non-rational forces that move and inspire us, and the idea that we are opaque rather than transparent, to ourselves, and not be able to fully self-knowledge or self-control, and psychoanalytic theory, it also challenges the rational, the human ego, and it shows that the ethical character of political and community may not be perfect, find the uncertainty in both the spiritual and political identity. Please do not assume that the unconscious is by a transgressive, or a conservative, but it is unreliable, sometimes it is beneficial for the rebellion or a rebellion, which was a strong and determined to defend the borders. Even though they are often in a complex environment and the psychoanalytic description of the unconscious and offer a feminist resource theory in both the political and the ontological investigation. Ontologically, the analysis shows a clear mental concept of, and the differences between men and women, and how we can live in our body and of our personality, and falsely informed the analysis, which is not reducible to either the social or the other of the categories. From a political point of view, the analysis provides a description of the forces, that will organize, disorganize, and the order of the relationship that the two of us. By providing insight into the formation of subjectivity, and animating fantasies, make use of the social life, the normal use, so it will also be the failure of the analysis of the enduring elements of a patriarchal social relations, including symbolic links, and the internal forces are used to support the identity, and the terminals of the sexual participants are in a relationship of domination and submission. Psychoanalytic feminism, and focus on the most important component of the society, the core of the differences between men and women in the community, helping to explain the final stage of male power, and enables feminist theorists to articulate possible correctives, problems, and ways to improve it, or ethical violations that are returned to politics and beyond, and not only in terms of the work to the public sphere.

CHAPTER ELEVEN

INTELLIGENCE AND CREATIVITY

Introduction

Intelligence is a broad concept that encompasses many different aspects of cognition. There has been a slew of theories proposed to explain what intelligence is and how it works. Sternberg's triarchic theory of intelligence emphasizes analytical, creative, and practical intelligence, while Gardner's theory claims that intelligence is made up of many variables. Other theories place a strong emphasis on emotional intelligence. A four-and-a-half-year-old child sits at the kitchen table with his father, who is reading him a new story. He begins to turn the page to resume reading, but the child cries, "Wait, Daddy!" before he can do so. "Pig, go! He exclaims, "Go!" as he points to the text on the new page. The father comes to a complete stop and faces his son. "Can you read that?" he asks. The child exclaims, "Yes, Daddy!" "Pig, go! "Go!" he exclaims once more, pointing to the words. This father was not actively teaching his kid to read, despite the boy's numerous questions about letters, words, and symbols that they encountered everywhere: in the car, in the store, on television. The father wanted to see what else his son could understand, so he decided to do an experiment. He scribbled a list of simple words on a sheet of blank paper: mom, dad, dog, bird, bed, truck, car, tree. He put the list in front of the child and asked him to read the words. He read carefully enough to pronounce the words bird and truck correctly. "Mom, dad, dog, bird, bed, truck, car, tree," he said. She inquires, "Did I do it, Daddy?" "Of course, you did! That's incredible." The father gave his son a warm hug and continued reading the pig story, all the while wondering if his son's abilities reflected extraordinary genius or just a normal pattern of linguistic development. Psychologists have wondered what intelligence is and how it might be assessed, much like the father in this story.

Classification of Intelligence

What precisely is intelligence? Researchers have revised their definitions of intelligence countless times since the beginning of psychology. A British psychologist named Charles Spearman believed that intelligence was made up of a single general component called g that could be measured and compared between people. Spearman emphasized the commonalities while downplaying the differences among various intellectual talents. Great thinkers like Aristotle, who lived long before modern psychology, held a similar attitude. Others believe that intelligence is more of a combination of skills than a single factor. In the 1940s, Raymond Cattell proposed a theory of intelligence that divided general intelligence into two categories: **crystallized intelligence** and **fluid intelligence.** Crystallized intellect possesses acquired information as well as the ability to regain it. When you learn, remember, and recall information, you use **crystallized intelligence**. In your education, you constantly display crystallized intelligence by demonstrating that you have mastered the content. Fluid intelligence is defined as the ability to recognize complicated relationships and solve problems. After being detoured into an unknown route owing to road construction, your fluid mind would be required to navigate your way home. **Fluid intelligence** helps you overcome intricate, abstract challenges in your daily life, whereas crystallized intelligence helps you overcome real, straightforward issues.

Practical intelligence: -

Sternberg's concept of practical intelligence is commonly referred to as "street smarts." Being practical involves utilizing knowledge based on your experiences to discover solutions that work in your daily life. This sort of intelligence appears to be distinct from traditional IQ; people with high practical intelligence scores may or may not have comparable creative and analytical intelligence scores.

The shootings at Virginia Tech demonstrate both high and low practical intelligences. During the incident, one girl left her class to go buy a Coke at an adjacent building. She wanted to return to class, but when she returned to her building after purchasing her drink, she noticed that the exit door had been locked from the inside. Instead of pondering about why there was a chain around the door knobs, she went to her class's window and snuck back inside. She may have thereby exposed herself to the gunman. Thankfully, she was not shot. On the other hand, a few of students were roaming around campus when they heard gunshots nearby. One friend said, "Let's go check it out and see what's going on." "No way," the other student said, "we have to get away from the gunshots." They did exactly what they said they were going to do. As a result, neither of them sustained any injuries. Although the student who crawled through the window shown considerable ingenuity, he lacked common sense. She'd have a low practical intelligence level. The student who persuaded his friend to run away from gunshots would have much greater practical intelligence.

Analytical intelligence: -

Analytical intelligence is inextricably tied to academic problem solving and computations. According to Sternberg, analytical intelligence is demonstrated by the ability to analyses, appraise, judge, compare, and contrast. It's customary to investigate the motives of the book's main characters or research the story's historical background when reading a classic novel for literature class, for example. In a science course such as anatomy, you must learn how the body uses various minerals in various human systems. To obtain a deeper understanding of this subject, you're use analytical intelligence. When confronted with a tough math problem, you would employ analytical intelligence to investigate numerous aspects of the problem before tackling it section by section.

Creative intelligence: -

An indication of creative intelligence is coming up with or inventing a solution to a problem or scenario. In this discipline, finding a creative solution to an unexpected problem, creating a beautiful work of art, or writing a well-developed short story are all instances of creativity. Consider yourself camping in the woods with some friends when you realize you've left your camp coffee pot at home. The employee who succeeds in preparing coffee for everyone in your company is regarded as having excellent creative intelligence.

Multiple intelligences theory: -

The Multiple Intelligences Theory was developed by Howard Gardner, a Harvard psychologist and Erik Erikson's former student. Gardner's idea, which has been improved for more than 30 years, is a more recent advance among intelligence hypotheses. Gardner believes that each person possesses at least eight intelligences. In most cases, a person excels in some of these eight intelligences while failing in others.

Gardner's concept is still in the works, and additional research is needed to demonstrate its empirical validity. Despite suggestions that Gardner just renamed what other theorists labelled "intelligence," his theories broaden the common definition of intelligence to embrace a larger variety of abilities "Intelligences" as "cognitive styles" (Morgan, 1996). Furthermore, traditional Gardner intelligence tests are extremely difficult to develop. Emotional intelligence is a term used to describe Gardner's interpersonal and intrapersonal intelligences.

Emotional Intelligence: -

Emotional intelligence is defined as the ability to detect and understand one's own and others' emotions, to display empathy, to interpret social interactions and cues, to manage one's own emotions, and to act in a culturally appropriate manner. Those with high emotional intelligence usually have well-developed social skills. According to Daniel Goleman, author of Emotional Intelligence: Why It Can Matter More Than IQ, emotional intelligence is a better predictor of success than standard intelligence. Emotional intelligence, on the other hand, has sparked a lot of debate, with experts pointing out inconsistencies in how it is defined and depicted, as well as casting doubt on the findings of research on a tough subject to quantify and analyses experimentally.

Intelligence can have diverse meanings and values in different cultures. Knowing how to fish and repair a boat is crucial if you live on a small island where the majority of people get their food through fishing from boats. If you were a fantastic fisherman, your coworkers would most certainly perceive you as intelligent. Your brilliance would undoubtedly be known around the island if you could also mend boats. Consider the customs of your own family.

In some cultures, working together as a group is highly appreciated. In these civilizations, the importance of group achievement outweighs the importance of individual achievement. When you visit a culture, your cultural intelligence, also known as cultural competency, is determined by how well you relate to its ideals.

Creativity

Someone is said to be creative if they come up with an innovative idea. An example is a creative solution to a difficult problem. But how can you tell if a notion or solution is innovative? Creativity is defined as the ability to conceive, invent, or discover new ideas, solutions, or possibilities. People who are extremely creative frequently have a strong understanding of a subject, work on it for years, contemplate new solutions, seek out the advice and support of other experts, and take risks. Despite the fact that creativity is often associated with the arts, it is a critical type of intelligence that drives people from all areas of life to try new things. Creativity may be found in every facet of life; from the way you decorate your home to a novel way of understanding how a cell works.

Although several definitions of creativity have been given by psychologists, the one most recently derived from the three criteria used by the United States Patent Office to decide whether an invention is patentable is likely the best.

The first criteria are originality. The concept must have a slim likelihood of becoming a reality. In reality, it should be distinguished on a frequent basis. Albert Einstein's special theory of relativity clearly fulfils this condition. There was no other scientist who thought of the idea.

What is Creative Process?

The flow of thoughts and actions that leads to the final shape of an idea is referred to as the creative process. The creative process necessitates critical thinking and problem-solving talents. From musicians to television producers, the five phases that creative people go through to bring their ideas to life are preparation, incubation, illumination, evaluation, and verification. The stages were first articulated by Graham Wallas, a social psychologist and co-founder of the London School of Economics, in his book The Art of Thought, which outlined the essential stages of the creative process.

The 5 stages of the Creative Process

While each artist approaches their work in their own unique way, most artists move through five stages subconsciously while working on their projects. Each of the five stages of the creative process leads to the next in a logical sequence. As you begin your own creative process, relax your mind and allow your ideas to develop through the five stages of creativity.

- **Preparation stage: -**

The initial step of the creative process entails preparation and idea development. This is when you gather information and perform study in order to come up with a novel idea. To develop divergent thinking, brainstorm and allow your thoughts wander, or write in a notebook; this will help you consider all conceivable routes to fleshing out your concept. The first stage of the process involves your brain accessing its memory bank to produce new ideas by drawing on previous information and experiences.

- **Incubation stage: -**

The second stage is to let go of your concept once you've finished actively thinking about it. Taking a step back from your concept before fleshing it out is an important part of creative thinking. You may focus on another project or take a break from the creative process entirely—whatever the case may be, you are not actively working on your idea. While it may appear counterproductive to walk away from your concept, it is a vital step in the process. Your narrative, song, or problem is incubating in the back of your mind during this period.

- **Illumination stage: -**

The lighting stage, often known as the "aha" moment, occurs when the "aha" moment occurs. As new connections emerge spontaneously, the light bulb goes out, and all of the information you've acquired comes together to present the solution to your problem. The answer to your creative quest comes to you in this third step. For example, you can get over writer's block by deciding out your story's ending. It may catch you off guard, but an idea has developed after the incubation period.

- **Evaluation stage: -**

During this stage, you evaluate the feasibility of your proposal and compare it to alternatives. This is also a moment for introspection, as you review your original notion or problem to evaluate if your solution matches your original vision. Market research may be conducted by business professionals to determine the viability of the concept. During this stage, you can either go back to the drawing board or keep going, confident in what you've created.

- **Verification stage: -**

This is when the creative process comes to a close. It's at this point when the real job begins. A physical object, an advertising campaign, a song, a novel, an architectural design—any item or object that you set out to produce, propelled by that initial thought that jumped into your head—could be your creative product. Now it's time to finish your design, bring your concept to life, and share it with the rest of the world.

Role of school in foresting creativity

A good classroom setting always includes some creative features, which make learning more engaging and participatory. The perfect combination of creativity and education allows pupils to be imaginative and learn new things. Students can improve their emotional and social abilities while also becoming better communicators. Creative classrooms have the potential to change the way students learn and apply what they learn in the real world. In truth, a student's emotional growth is aided by artistic expression. Let's take a look at how vital creativity is in today's classroom and the benefits it provides.

- **Learn with fun: -**

Students can learn while having a good time in a creative classroom. Teaching methods like storytelling and skits allow students to learn without feeling rushed.

Students are usually up for a good time, and incorporating creative activities into the curriculum increases their enthusiasm for learning.

Teachers should develop this quality in pupils as early as the primary grades, inspiring them to believe in their own inventiveness.

Fun team building exercises can be designed to encourage creative thinking in groups and to teach people how to accept the ideas of others.

- **Freedom of expression: -**

In contrast to traditional teaching approaches, creative classrooms allow them to express themselves. Students get the opportunity to come out of their shells and participate in debates, classroom discussions, and field trips. They feel wonderful and happy because of their freedom of expression.

Contributing to the learning sessions provides them a sense of accomplishment as well. A creative learning technique opens them up to the puzzles that come their way and offers them a sense of accomplishment and pride.

- **Emotional development: -**

A child's emotional development depends on their ability to express themselves creatively. Importantly, this must occur in their lower classes as well, so that they grow up by responding appropriately to events in their environment.

They have the freedom to explore their surroundings and discover new things because of their creativity.

Students will always appreciate a school environment that allows them to explore freely without being restricted. They will gain confidence when they are able to express their actual emotions in a creative manner in their classrooms.

- **Enhances thinking capability: -**

Students' innovative thinking abilities can be stimulated through creativity. In the middle of demanding curriculum schedules, teachers advocate activities such as open-ended questions, creative team building activities, brainstorming sessions, and discussions.

Some teachers utilize these strategies deftly to teach difficult concepts in a way that students like. Puppet performances, for example, will keep students engaged in the learning sessions, and the flow of images in their minds will provide them with the pleasure of creativity. They will be able to come up with inventive replies to the open-ended questions, which will open up a world of imaginative thinking for them.

- **Reduced stress and anxiety: -**

It relieves a lot of tension from pupils when some time is made aside for creativity in between all of the tough study sessions. This joy keeps them relaxed and minimizes their anxiety, allowing them to prepare well for exams and perform well on them.

Including more hands-on learning and allowing for visual reflection will have a significant impact. Encouraging fruitful debates and making the classroom arrangement more adaptable are all important factors in creating a creative learning environment.

- **Boost's problem-solving skills: -**

Children's problem-solving skills can be stimulated through brainstorming sessions using puzzles.

Creativity may drastically affect how students approach an issue, and it can leave them feeling incredibly positive after participating in creative teaching sessions.

In order to help kids, think outside the box and be more inventive and original, creative problem solving can be encouraged in the classroom.

Students will reinterpret the issues or possibilities in this manner, and the answers or replies will be more imaginative.

- **Improves focus and attention: -**

A lower-class child's average attention or concentration span is only a few minutes. Traditional instructional methods would bore them, and they might lose interest in the middle.

Incorporating creative teaching tactics such as storytelling and skits will undoubtedly boost their focus and attention, resulting in more effective study time.

Playing memory games, taking regular breaks and intervals to encourage creativity, and creating a flexible classroom environment will help them enhance their attention span significantly.

- **Better communication: -**

They can improve their attention span greatly by playing memory games, taking regular breaks and intervals to foster creativity, and providing a flexible classroom environment. Classroom arguments not only help children think creatively, but they also help them comprehend and accept the perspectives of others. This type of collaborative creative experience encourages kids to open up and become better communicators.

- **Follow passion: -**

It is critical for a student to pursue their passions in addition to succeeding in academics if they are to be successful in life. A good classroom setting should allow pupils to pursue their interests in music, dance, poetry, sketching, and other forms of art.

This makes kids feel happy, which allows them to approach academics with an open mind.

Setting aside time for such activities can help kids improve their creative abilities as well as their academic abilities. Students who make the best use of these chances can graduate with honors.

- **Future opportunities: -**

Charts that depict the goals, along with timetables, can help students keep track of their progress in a challenging classroom. Students gain the foundation for how successful they can be when they grow up in the school.

The abilities and confidence students develop throughout their school years will have a significant impact on how they progress in their careers.

In reality, those with a creative skill set have an advantage over those with a purely academic skill set in terms of triggering future chances. During the knockout stages, they are allowed to express themselves, and how they show themselves is extremely important in this competitive period.

- **Innovative mindset: -**

Two common creative teaching tactics that help students develop an innovative mentality are open-ended questions and classroom debates. Students are given the opportunity to think critically about the situation or subject at hand and to come up with novel solutions.

The amicable classroom conversations also help kids think critically about other people's ideas and contributions in order to create something new. Lower-class pupils can benefit from a lively classroom environment that is colorful rather than black and white, and teachers might make an attempt to include some comedy in between sessions.

- **Drive Lifelong Learning: -**

A person with a creative mindset has a constant desire to learn new things, which allows them to enjoy the wonderful sense of lifelong learning.

This would keep them interested and busy throughout the day, allowing them to stay young at all times. An inquisitive mind is constantly eager to learn more, and creative classrooms can help children develop a curious attitude in unique ways.

With the rising mobile industry, education apps are on the rise, and there are several fantastic apps that encourage creativity, such as Doodle Buddy, 123D Sculpt, Audacity, and GarageBand.

It is, however, the responsibility of a good teacher to bring the correct mix of creativity into the classroom and to bring out the best in students.

The pleasure of creativity also contributes significantly to improved health, allowing them to continue to flourish academically and in the field of creative.

Conclusion of intelligence and creativity

The ability to acquire and apply knowledge is how intelligence is traditionally characterized. In testing situations, one's capacity to use historical information is used to determine one's Intelligence Quotient (IQ).

The ability to come up with new ideas through a mental process of connecting existing notions is referred to as creativity. The ideas don't have to be revolutionary (a common misperception about creative thinking), but they do have to be novel to the thinker.

Intelligence does have a role in creative thinking, but not in the way you may imagine.

In general, your IQ is determined by your capacity to interpret data and give solutions, regardless of the situation. IQ is extremely significant in mathematics and basic sciences since it displays your capacity to recall concepts and apply them to similar issues. If I tell you that two plus two equals four, you should be able to deduce that four plus four equals double the original answer (ideally).

This fact alone indicates intelligence's link to creativity, which is critical for not just understanding but also increasing creative thinking. Another crucial feature of intelligence is the ability to effectively filter solutions.

If you're good at obtaining knowledge (say, by reading, lectures, or watching YouTube videos) and putting that knowledge to good use, but not so good at filtering through solutions, you'll come up with good ideas, but it'll take a long time. Those with high cognitive levels, on the other hand, can quickly sift through concepts.

To be creative, you must apply previous knowledge to a new scenario and quickly filter through the various possibilities. Of course, existing knowledge is something that anyone with an IQ over a certain level can acquire. It appears that the intelligence number is somewhere around 100.

To summaries, expert creatives do not have to be smarter than the typical person. They simply do three things better than anyone else: they have more experiences, they reflect on their experiences more frequently, and when pursuing potential solutions to problems or projects, they simply work harder with the ideas they generate (whereas everyone else gives up after evaluating just one or two possible ideas, or by letting their inner critic prevent them from exploring more).

CHAPTER TWELVE

INTELLIGENCE THEORIES: A HOLISTIC FRAMEWORK FOR FACILITATING THE LEARNING PROCESS

Introduction:

Intelligence is the ability to both acquire and apply knowledge and a set of skills required for executing the knowledge from the abstract state to that of practical utility. This involves inculcating an ability to deal with knotty situations, manipulate a difficult environment to human advantage and verify theorems and theories in the realm of objective manifestation of the same. Perception, attention, memory, language and planning are vital preconditions for the successful operability of intelligence in the human domain. Creativity is concerned with inventiveness and originality of invention. Naturally, the creative function requires imagination, ingenuity and vision. Therefore, creativity is a phenomenon by which something of value and utility is formed, at the level of ideation and autonomy. Both intelligence and creativity are significant concerns for effecting a guided visualisation, adaptive performance and brainstorming activity, so that a plan of action takes a material shape, especially if it concerns the learning process.

The study of human intelligence dates back to the late 1800s when Sir Francis Galton (the cousin of Charles Darwin) became one of the first people to study intelligence.

Galton was interested in the concept of a gifted individual, so he created a lab to measure reaction times and other physical characteristics to test his hypothesis that intelligence is a general mental ability that is a produce of biological evolution (hello, Darwin!).

Galton theorized that because quickness and other physical attributes were evolutionarily advantageous, they would also provide a good indication of general mental ability (Jensen, 1982).

Thus, Galton operationalized intelligence as reaction time.

Operationalization is an important process in research that involves defining an unmeasurable phenomenon (such as intelligence) in measurable terms (such as reaction time), allowing the concept to be studied empirically (Crowthre-Heyck, 2005).

Galton's study of intelligence in the laboratory setting and his theorization of the heritability of intelligence paved the way for decades of future research and debate in this field.

Defining the Praxis of Intelligence:

Intelligence is defined as the capacity or ability of a person to acquire information, accommodate and process it and then apply it in appropriate contexts. It is basically that trait that is helpful in managing and facing real life situations. The study of human intelligence dates back to the late 1800s when Sir Francis Galton became one of the first person to study Intelligence. Intelligence aid humans to make decisions, solve problems, formulate logical reasoning, innovate, understand and plan things in the rightful manner and follow a patterned self-awareness with improved levels of motivation and cognitive capabilities. David Wechsler in 1944 defined Intelligence as the aggregate or global capacity of an individual to act purposefully, to think rationally and to deal effectively with his environment. Piaget in 1952 in a similar tone viewed Intelligence as the ability to adapt to one's surroundings.

Factors Contributing to Intelligence:

The most common question which arises is that whether or not there are any particular factors which contributes to intelligence in a person. To understand it, one must know that the combined functioning of a large number of genes generally contributes to Intelligence in a person. Intelligence is also determined to a large extent by the environmental factors surrounding a person. For instance, it has often been noted that a child, with sufficient availability of resources, improved nutrition, proper parenting, tutoring and hailing from a good family backdrop is naturally intelligent and prospers in other major aspects of life.

Concept of Mental Age:

A very close concept associated with Intelligence is Mental Age. It is nothing but a determining factor of how good an individual can utilise his cognitive abilities at a specific age, compared to the average intellectual functioning of a person of his age. While chronological age of a person is based on calendar date as to when that person is born, the mental age of the same person is purely dependent on his or her intellectual development. For most people, the mental and chronological age are the same and they are said to belong to the average intelligence group. Retarded children have mental ages lower than their chronological age, while gifted children, on the contrary have mental ages higher than the chronological age.

Intelligence Quotient (IQ):

The IQ of a child or adult is normally measured for educational or job placement and is conducted by means of standardised intelligent test. The score of such tests is basically obtained by dividing a person's mental age score (derived from the test) by the person's chronological age, and then multiplying the fraction by hundred. IQ = Mental Age/Chronological Age * 100.

Intelligence, so to say, is a trait which varies from individual to individual, from age to age and from one context to another. Surveys over time have revealed that a majority of people holds average intelligence, a few are very bright and some are very dull.

Theories of Intelligence:

Some researchers argue that intelligence is a general ability, whereas others make the assertion that intelligence comprises specific skills and talents. Psychologists contend that intelligence is genetic, or inherited, and others claim that it is largely influenced by the surrounding environment.

As a result, psychologists have developed several contrasting theories of intelligence as well as individual tests that attempt to measure this very concept.

There are several theories of Intelligence, upholding a concept that is different from the rest. The question which often arises about Intelligence is that whether there is any general intelligence or a multiple set of the same. Opinions have always differed among psychologists regarding this matter and so some of the important theories are discussed below:-

Spearman's Two Factor Theory –

General intelligence, also known as g factor, refers to a general mental ability that, according to Spearman, underlies multiple specific skills, including verbal, spatial, numerical and mechanical.

Charles Spearman, an English psychologist, established the two-factor theory of intelligence back in 1904 (Spearman, 1904). To arrive at this theory, Spearman used a technique known as factor analysis.

Factor analysis is a procedure through which the correlation of related variables are evaluated to find an underlying factor that explains this correlation.

In the case of intelligence, Spearman noticed that those who did well in one area of intelligence tests (for example, mathematics), also did well in other areas (such as distinguishing pitch; Kalat, 2014).

In other words, there was a strong correlation between performing well in math and music, and Spearman then attributed this relationship to a central factor, that of general intelligence (g).

Charles Spearman in 1904 gave his theory that intelligence in a person is typically composed of two factors:-

*G-Factor – which is the inborn ability in an individual and is constant. It is also called the General Ability.

*S-Factor – which is acquired from the environment surrounding the individual. It is also known as the Specific Ability.

The aggregate Intelligence that a person possesses is typically the sum total of the G-Factor and the S-Factor, according to Spearman.

Thorndike's Multifactor Theory–

Rejecting the proposition of General ability, Thorndike believed that that individuals require a diverse range of abilities in order to accomplish basic tasks, which he described as Intelligence. He classified the attributes of Intelligence into four categories which are follows:-

a) Level – The toughness or level of difficulty of a task that the individual would be able to solve.

b) Range – Refers to the quantity or number of assignments or tasks that the individual would be able to handle at any given degree of difficulty.

c) Area – The number of proper responses at each level which the individual is capable of giving.

d) Speed – Indicates the promptness with which the individual can respond to the enlisted items.

Thurstone's Group Factor Theory of Intelligence –

Thurstone (1938) challenged the concept of a g-factor. After analyzing data from 56 different tests of mental abilities, he identified a number of primary mental abilities that comprise intelligence, as opposed to one general factor.

The seven primary mental abilities in Thurstone's model are verbal comprehension, verbal fluency, number facility, spatial visualization, perceptual speed, memory, and inductive reasoning (Thurstone, as cited in Sternberg, 2003).

Thurstone believed that Intelligence is a cluster of abilities. Each of these abilities has its own primary factor, thereby contributing a functional unity to the group. Thurstone has basically classified six primary factors, each of which is independent of the others, and they are as follows.

a) The Number Factor (N) – The ability to solve numerical problems with promptness and accuracy.

b) The Verbal Factor (V) – Measured by tests like reading comprehension and vocabulary, this factor involves a person's ability to understand verbal material.

c) The Space Factor (S) – The aptitude of estimating and understanding shapes and patterns typically concerns the Space Factor. For instance, the children's ability to fit together pieces of puzzle to form a coordinated structure, comes under this factor.

d) Memory (M) - It is the cognitive capacity to memorize things quickly with the ability to recall, assimilate and associate previously learned materials.

e) The Word Fluency Factor (W) – Refers to the individual's stock of vocabulary and his sheer ability to think of isolated words with promptness and precision.

f) The Reasoning Factor (R) - The capacity of an individual to decide upon and solve situations with sufficient logic and reason coms under the reasoning factor.

Although Thurstone did not reject Spearman's idea of general intelligence altogether, he instead theorized that intelligence consists of both general ability and a number of specific abilities, paving the way for future research that examined the different forms of intelligence.

Cattell's Theory of Intelligence –

Psychologist Raymond Cattell suggested two forms of Intelligence which are mainly used by pupils in handling problems or situations. They are –

a) Fluid Intelligence – represents intelligence in a human being that is inherited. Fluid Intelligence is mainly helpful in solving puzzles and using problem solving strategies in specific situations.

b) Crystallised Intelligence – that intellectual ability which may not be inherited but obtained through learning and experience over the years. It increases with age and with the prospective years of experience that a person is able to gather in his or her lifetime.

5. Sternberg's Triarchic Theory - Sternberg proposed of three types of Intelligence which pupils normally possesses. They are –

a) Practical Intelligence – The capability of a person to react justifiably in their external environment and behave in successful ways is called Practical Intelligence.

b) Creative Intelligence – The utilisation of existing knowledge by an individual to carve new methods in handling or coping with problems with a quintessential creative approach comes under Creative Intelligence.

c) Analytical Intelligence – It is the Intelligence which is used by pupils mainly in academic situations. It involves the ability to analyse, evaluate, compare, contrast and react to different aspect of the problem with a degree of precision and is called Analytical Intelligence.

Guildford's Structure of Intellect:

Following the work of Thurstone, American psychologist Howard Gardner built off the idea that there are multiple forms of intelligence.

He proposed that there is no single intelligence, but rather distinct, independent multiple intelligences exist, each representing unique skills and talents relevant to a certain category.

Gardner (1983, 1987) initially proposed seven multiple intelligences: linguistic, logical-mathematical, spatial, musical, bodily-kinesthetic, interpersonal, and intrapersonal, and he has since added naturalist intelligence.

Guildford described Intelligence as a systematic collection of a composite number of abilities which are essential for processing different kinds of information. He used a Factor Analytic technique approach. Guildford believed that an individual's test performance can be traced back to underlying mental abilities or factors which are basically 180 in number and they can be categorized o organised in three broad dimensions: Content, Product and Operations in his 'Structure of Intellect' or SOI Model. The basic dimensions are further classified into several sub categories.

i) **Content Dimension** – The Content Dimension is divided into four sub categories which are as follows:-

a) Visual – refers to the information which is perceived through seeing whereby the retina forms an image.

b) Auditory – it is the information perceived through learning a piece of verbal information.

c) Symbolic – the information that is read through different symbols or signs representing particular things.

d) Semantic – concerned with information which is verbal or written or even present in one's mind.

e) Behavioural – refers to the information that is perceived through individual acts.

ii) **Operations Dimension** – The five sub categories of Operations Dimension are as follows:-

a) Cognition- It is the basic awareness of a person involving the general ability to understand and comprehend the meaning of things.

b) Memory – It is the capacity of memorizing and retaining information.

c) Evaluation – It is the judgemental approach of an individual to determine whether a piece of information or answer is constant, valid or reliable.

d) Divergent Production – The process of giving composite or more than one solutions to a single problem.

e) Convergent Production – The process of solving a particular problem with a single and unique solution.

iii)**Product Dimension** – This is the dimension which applies particular operations to specific contents. Products are further classified into the following six types:-

a) Unit – Concerns with a single item of information.

b) Class – Concerns with a set of items concerning some attributes.

c) Relation – Typically concerns with the connection between items or variables such as associations, sequences, analogies, similarities or opposites.

d) System – Refers to the intricate network of items with their interacting parts.

e) Transformation – It is the change or conversions of perspectives or mutation to an organised form of knowledge. For example- reversing the order of letters to transform it in a word.

f) Implication – Refers to the closure part and is concerned with the inferences, consequences or anticipations of knowledge.

And although this theory has widely captured the attention of the psychology community and greater public, it does have its faults.

There have been few empirical studies that actually test this theory, and this theory does not account for other types of intelligence beyond the ones Gardner lists (Sternberg, 2003).

Howard Gardner's Theory of Multiple Intelligences:

In his book "Frames of Mind: The Theory of Multiple Intelligences", psychologist Howard Gardner suggested that all people have different kind of 'intelligences'. A person, in order to achieve the full range of his or her abilities, cannot just bank on mere intellectual capacity according to him, but rather have to seek help of many kind of intelligences. The utilisation of such intelligences depend on the specific areas on which a particular person is strong and competent. There are nine kind of intelligences enlisted by Gardner all of which are discussed in the following:-

i) Linguistic Intelligence – The sensitivity of a person to perceive spoken and written languages, with the ability to learn and use languages appropriately in the correct context comes under Linguistic Intelligence. People with such intelligences are generally authors or good orators.

ii) Logical-Mathematical intelligence – Refers to the capacity to complete and analyse logical problems, investigate and solve them based on adequate reasoning and the aptitude to carry out mathematical calculations with accuracy and promptness.

iii) Spatial Intelligence – The knowledge about perception of space, whether confined or wide, comes under this category. For example-navigators and pilots have to sense wide spaces and dimensions whereas sculptors or architects have to manage small spaces to give accuracy to their portrayal. Both can be said, thus, to possess spatial intelligence.

iv) Bodily-Kinaesthetic Intelligence – The ability to solve problems by using one's body, parts of the body or mouth or even through unison of mind and body falls under this category.

v) Musical Intelligence – Some people excel overwhelmingly in their musical abilities. They can compose several musical tracks and can perform songs with self-patterned tones or beats. For example, most participants of reality shows in music in the Television comes under this category.

vi)Interpersonal Intelligence – The capacity of an effective interaction or communication with other social members through understanding their choices, desires and intentions is termed as Interpersonal Intelligence. For example, great leaders of the country like Mahatma Gandhi, Jawaharlal Nehru, Swami Vivekananda and other are examples of such.

vii) Intrapersonal intelligence – The most important aspect in an individual's life is self-assessment and understanding by which one should have a clear cut concept of one's own capacities, limitations or strengths. By having a clear perception of one's own self, an individual would not confuse with what he or she himself wants to achieve and do in life and thus can regulate things appropriately. This is called Intrapersonal Intelligence by Gardner.

viii) Naturalist Intelligence – It refers to the conception of the environment in which the individual resides. Some people expertise in the recognition of various species of flora and fauna and loves to be involved in gaining knowledge about them and thus are said to possess Naturalist Intelligence.

ix) Existential Intelligence – This type of intelligence is added by Gardner much laterand refers to some people's knowledge and yearning to handle deep seated existential questions about life and afterlife such as 'Why do we exist?', 'What is the meaning of life?', 'What happens after death?' and so on.

Gardner was of the opinion that individuals can use one intelligence or a combination of two or three intelligences at a time in order to handle life situations depending on his ability or capacity.

Daniel Goleman's Theory of Emotional Intelligence:

It is commonly been noted that there are a large number of pupils who have high IQ and excel in academic life and other facets of life but cannot navigate and understand their own mind and thus fights a conflicting battle with their own self throughout their lives. It is basically at this critical juncture that cognition and emotion should meet and work as a unified whole to develop and facilitate an individual's capacity of reasoning, resilience, empathy, stress management, communication with the outside world and the like. This is called Emotional Intelligence.

John D Mayer and Peter Salovey in 1990 first coined the term 'Emotional Intelligence' and described it as a form of social intelligence involving the ability of a person to regulate one's own feeling and emotions as well as others. In 1990, Daniel Goleman took over the concept and developed his book named 'Emotional Intelligence'.

Emotionally intelligent people can cope up with any crisis situation in a more effective manner than people with less Emotional intelligence. For instance, while an upsetting movie can totally disrupt pupil with less Emotional Intelligence, Emotionally Intelligent pupils seem to be less affected and cope up with the upsetting situation in less time for they have the required logic and reason for handling any kind of situations loaded with discrepancies.

Goleman identified five dimensions of Emotional Intelligence which are as follows:-

- Self-Awareness – an individual would first know his or her self properly and identify his or her own strengths or limitations which is the self-awareness of that individual.
- Self-regulation – Indicated qualitative restraint and control over one's emotional behaviour and channelize oneself in a proper manner.
- Motivation – Emotionally intelligent people are found to be self-motivated and tends to care little about external incentives like money or recognition.
- Empathy - The sociability of a person blooms only when he is genuinely empathetic towards the other members of the society and feels for them on a genuine level.
- Social Skills – Emotionally intelligent people generally has improved social skillsbased on mutual trust and respect for the other people in the community with whom they live.

Triarchic Theory of Intelligence

Just two years later, in 1985, Robert Sternberg proposed a three-category theory of intelligence, integrating components that were lacking in Gardner's theory. This theory is based on the definition of intelligence as the ability to achieve success based on your personal standards and your sociocultural context.

According to the triarchic theory, intelligence has three aspects: analytical, creative, and practical (Sternberg, 1985).

- Analytical intelligence, also referred to as componential intelligence, refers to intelligence that is applied to analyze or evaluate problems and arrive at solutions. This is what a traditional IQ test measure.

- Creative intelligence is the ability to go beyond what is given to create novel and interesting ideas. This type of intelligence involves imagination, innovation and problem-solving.
- Practical intelligence is the ability that individuals use to solve problems faced in daily life, when a person finds the best fit between themselves and the demands of the environment. Adapting to the demands environment involves either utilizing knowledge gained from experience to purposefully change oneself to suit the environment (adaptation), changing the environment to suit oneself (shaping), or finding a new environment in which to work (selection).

Emotional Intelligence

Emotional Intelligence is the "ability to monitor one's own and other people's emotions, to discriminate between different emotions and label them appropriately, and to use emotional information to guide thinking and behavior" (Salovey and Mayer, 1990).

Emotional intelligence is important in our everyday lives, seeing as we experience one emotion or another nearly every second of our lives. You may not associate emotions and intelligence with one another, but in reality, they are very related.

Emotional intelligence refers to the ability to recognize the meanings of emotions and to reason and problem-solve on the basis of them (Mayer, Caruso, & Salovey, 1999). The four key components of emotional Intelligence are (i) self-awareness, (ii) self-management, (iii) social awareness, and (iv) relationship management.

CHAPTER THIRTEEN

CONCEPT OF CREATIVITY ,ITS PROCESS & ROLE OF SCHOOL IN FOSTERING CREATIVITY

Introduction

Consider all the living beings of earth, they breathe, manage their food, arrange for shelter and reproduce to maintain their generations. Among them, the man enjoys a superior place, they are logical animals, they can differentiate between right and wrong, they can learn the things and they can work to improve their life standards. All these humans are important but the credit of making the life of all human beings better and more comfortable goes to those who have the ability to think differently, to create something new and to do innovations for making the human life easier. **James Watt** invented the steam engine, **William Cullen** invented the refrigerator and **Martin Cooper** invented the mobile phone; all these innovations make the life of humans comfortable but the question arises what ability they possess different from others that make them capable to think in a totally different way? The answeris "Creativity", the ability to think out of the box and find out a new solution to a problem from the available resources.

Creativity

Some children can sing well without any training, some start dancing well at an early years of age, some can draw the paintings easily and some can solve complex mathematical problems in seconds, each child has some special ability. But some children are totally different from all others. They show extraordinary imagination power, live in fantasies, have variety of unusual thoughts and try to rearrange and create the new toy from their old broken toys. These children are called '**creative children**' and their ability to imagine something new is known as creativity. Creativity is the ability to think away from the traditional pattern, to create new ideas and to discover new possibilities. It is actually a kind of intelligence that makes a man capable to innovate something new and valuable. Creative children may combine two or more unrelated words or ideas and give a new answer or novel response to a situation. In a layman's term when an artist create a new painting, a poet composes a poetry and an inventor invents something new; all the creations represent the creativity of their creator and creator through his creation reprsents his unusual and innovative thoughts. **Spearman (1931)** defined creativity as 'the process of human mind to create new concepts by transforming relations and thereby generating new correlations. '**Stagner & Karwoski (1973)** states that 'creativity implies the production of totally or partially novel identity.' **Skinner in 1968** postulates that 'creative thinking means that the predictions and/or inferences for the individual are new, original, unusual. The creative thinker is one who explores new areas and makes new observation, new prediction and new inferences.' From these definitions mentioned above it is clear thatcreativity involves creating, inventing or regenerating something new, unusual, unique and useful. It is different from intelligence as it is not limited upto the acceptance and application of knowledge rather it involves divergent thinking, it has originality and its result is something innovative.

Elements of Creativity

Gillford (1986) states that creativity involves divergent thinking which emphasizes on following four components -

Fluency – Most significant indicator of creativity is plenty of ideas. A normal person when thinks about solving a problem or searches answer to a question, he may find two or three solutions or answers but a creative person can think of many solutions effortlessly.

Flexibility – Creative people perform divergent thinking. They have plenty of ideas but these ideas are not similar instead creative children have the ability to produce a varied mix of ideas.

Originality – Creative ideas have uniqueness, novelty and newness. Creative people have the ability to generate new and rare solution to the problem that nobody has listened before.

Elaboration – The last element of creativity is elaboration. Creative individuals have the ability to elaborate the thought in order to modify or expand upon an idea.

Process of Creativity

Creativity is not genetic in nature. Some children get that as a gift of God. But the generation and development of creative idea in the mind of creative child follows successive stages. **Graham Wallas** was the first who discussed four stages of creativity in his book **'Art of Thought'** in **1926**. This model of creativity is also known as **'Wallas Model of Creativity'**. According to him in the process of generation of a creative idea, mind of creative person passes through following four different stages –

1. **Preparation** – Preparation is the conscious stage of creativity in which creative mind gathers the related information. Creative idea is not popped up in vacuum but it is generated in response to problem or need. According to Wallas in this stage creative mind identifies the problem and investigates it to collect all the information related to this and starts its preparation to find a novel solution to a problem.

1. **Incubation** – Incubation is the unconscious stage of creativity, which is also known as **'walk away stage'** or **'absence of activity stage'** where after analyzing and collecting all the information when mind doesn't find any idea or solution it starts working somewhere else but the knowledge remains active in unconscious mind.

3. **Illumination** – In third stage of creativity **'Eureka!!'** or 'aha' moment occurs in which mind experiences sudden appearance of solution. This stage is the most classic characteristic of a creative person. All the information collected in the stage of preparation remains active in unconscious mind during incubation period and all of a sudden **'moment of insight'** occurs and new idea or solution to the problem strikes in the mind of creative person.

4. **Verification** – Getting the solution of the problem is not sufficient. It needs verification that whether the idea or solution to a problem appears suddenly in the mind is right or wrong or need any modification. And when mind verifiesthe idea and finds it relevant and valid, the person shares his idea with others. But creative mind is never satisfied, it starts processing other information.

Role of School in Fostering Creativity

School is a second home to learners where they spend most of their time with the peers learning various life lessons, developing skills and inculcating values and virtues. School is the foundation on which the teacher builds up the future of the learners shaping their behaviour and imparting knowledge. Teacher is not only an individual who performs his duties or a professional who discharges his services, teacher is like a gardener who plants the saplings, waters them, nurtures and nourishes them to grow into a robust and strong tree. A teacher devotes and dedicates himself entirely to the service of nation by ensuring the holistic growth and development of its future leaders that he creates in his classrooms. School is the workplace of a teacher where he toils day in and day out. School has a crucial role to play in the development of competencies, skills, ethics and creativity in the young learners.

School education and creativity

In his praised talk on Technology, Entertainment and Design (TED), Sir Ken Robinson asked a question: Do schools kill creativity? This has been a much argued issue throughout the history of formal schooling. There are those who maintain that school is actually a place that promotes creativity through arts, music, play and problemsolving in various parts of curriculum and thus advances it rather than extinguishes it. This includes a footnote that many children would never engage in these creative activities unless they were given opportunities to do so in school. Elementary schools have traditionally been places where more creative action and thinking have occurred than in further stages of education.

But then there are those, like Sir Ken Robinson, Seymour Sarason, Shlomo Sharan and Robert Sternberg, who take a more critical stance on that question. Their main argument is that as young people progress through their school education, their genuine interest and innate curiosity in exploring the world around them gradually decline and they seem to be educated out of creativity (Robinson, 2009; Sarason, 1990; Sharan & Chin

Tan, 2008; Sternberg, 2006). This happens, they say, because much of what young people do in school is driven by an idea of 'the right answer' and one standard way to get it. The older young people get, the less they have courage to try other ways of thinking and the more they try to avoid being wrong. How much of this is directly due to school and how much it is just a normal course of development remains a disputable issue. Most people connect creativity in schools to subjects that naturally invite one's creative talent to be utilised. Therefore music, visual arts, drama and design are seen as domains that develop students' creative abilities. Rather interestingly, within arts in schools drawing and music are higher in the hierarchy than drama and dance. Therefore it is common in many countries that as the call for more creativity in school education is responded, it means more lesson time for drawing and music. The notion that many more education policymakers and practitioners need to accept is that there are many of us who need to move to be able to think and to create new ideas. Too much deskwork and listening to a teacher is not good for nurturing creativity. As we have shown elsewhere, a vast majority of students' time in school is spent sitting quietly and receiving information from teachers (Sahlberg & Boce, in print).

In our field research we found that in a typical first year upper secondary school lesson there is less than 30 seconds time in total for student-initiated talk. This makes any creative thinking or behaviour in such classrooms practically impossible. Thinking that developing creative thinking and skills is a business of drawing and music in school is, however, a rather narrow view of creativity. If creativity means having original ideas that are useful, it can relate to any activity in school and any subject in curriculum. And it certainly should. Students can engage in creative learn ing in sciences, foreign languages and mathematics, among many others. All teachers can teach almost anything in a creative way so that students need to do things in new ways and come up with novel ideas. But many teachers find this a real challenge for two main reasons: first, many of them think that they are not themselves creative and cannot therefore teach creatively; second, even more teachers think that their own teaching in school should be more creative but they are forced to follow standardised procedures to guarantee that students learn what is included in curricula and textbooks. I will say more about these two points next.

Everyone has some creative talent

If you ask people if they think they are creative persons only very few will answer unconditionally 'yes'. Indeed, most of us think that we do not qualify to be someone who could be named a creative person. I often meet individuals who claim that they are not good at anything. Again, creative people are normally those who paint, sing, dance or invent new things. This is closely linked to a conception that some of have creative talent and most us don't, as Robinson (2009) eloquently describes in his book The Element. Without forcefully challenging this conception it is unlikely that there will be more creative teaching and learning in schools.

If we define creativity in terms of people's artistic abilities we could safely confirm the conventional view that not all have creative talent. What seems to be true with many of us is that we rarely find out in school what our real natural talents are. In other words, we go through our initial education in school without realising what we really can do and where we excel. We find our passion elsewhere afterwards: in our hobbies, through work or in family life. Many people can create unbelievable things that they never thought they could do in school. A number of world known scientists, dancers and thinkers discovered their natural talent only after leaving school. Ex-Beatles Paul McCartney, celebrated choreographer Gillian Lynne and Nobel Prize-winning economist Paul Samuelson are examples of those who think that their schools successfully kept them away from what they really are rather than helping then to discover their true talents (Robinson, 2009). Many of them left school with a belief that they, like most of their peers, had no special creative abilities.

Not the 21st-century education system

Appeal for more creativity and innovation in education comes, not from the education community but from a global economical emergency, technological advancement and the urgent need for change. The main reason is that all national education systems are based on two underlying models: an economic model and an intellectual model. These two systems models are operationally linked to each other. The economic model of education is industrialism that views education as the production of knowledge and skills for predetermined purposes and markets (Robinson, 2009). Teaching and learning are steered by the principles of efficiency and rationalism and are therefore sequenced into manageable units and programmed by a predetermined schedule. The logic of the economic model of education is based on a belief in competition and information as the key drivers of educational improvement — just like they drive efficiency and productivity in market economies. The intellectual model, in turn, views intelligence primarily as an academic ability that is dominated by memory and rote academic skills rather than by broader intellectual, interpersonal or creative processes.

This model assumes that intelligence can and should be measured to determine individuals' educational progress (Sahlberg, 2010). The problem today is that the economic model is outdated and the intellectual model is inadequate for the needs of the unpredictably changing innovation-driven society. Education reforms rarely attempt to challenge seriously these two underlying assumptions of school organisation. Instead, education policies today aim at raising standards, extending time for learning or having more computers in schools. These particular efforts will remain an insufficient means of improving the quality of education unless the basic economic and the intellectual models of education are reconsidered. This has been a long-standing claim by Seymour Sarason (1990), for example, who has predicted that most educational reforms will fail unless the culture of the school will become the locus of change.

Barriers: competition, standardisation, test-based accountability

In many countries teachers have autonomy in their own classrooms to decide how teaching and learning is arranged. Curricula, textbooks and educational guidelines normally stipulate the content and schedule for teaching but methodology is, in most cases, up to a teacher to decide. The emergence of the global educational reform movement, or germ, has brought to many education systems new elements that seem also to regulate how teachers design teaching and learning in their classrooms (Hargreaves & Shirley, 2009; Sahlberg, 2010). Some of these global trends are particularly interesting and important when creativity and innovation in schools are concerned. Next I will discuss three barriers to more creativity in schools followed by three enablers that might help to reshape teaching and learning in an innovation society.

Barrier 1: Competition as the main driver of educational improvement A particular approach to educational change is based on a belief in competition and information as the key drivers of educational improvement. The logic of this marketorientation is rather straightforward. It is built on the belief that competition — as it does in the market economy — drives efficiency and improvement, and can be applied to schools as well, so that competition among schools would lead to better outcomes for students. In order for schools to compete, individual schools would require much more autonomy. Parents would need to be able to choose the schools their children attended. And finally, in order to choose, parents and the public would require measures of student achievement and education quality to compare and guide their choice of schools, based on a single national curriculum. Competition has forced schools and teachers to look for new aspects in their work. But not so much the way that teachers teach and students learn but rather how schools, districts and entire education systems gain an advantage over other schools in the race for the best students, resources and public reputation. Many schools in England, the United States and even in Finland have recreated their educational profiles. However, the main rationale for doing so is not student learning but competition for resources and better human resources.

Barrier 2: Standardisation of teaching and learning Globalisation has increased competition but also collaboration (Sahlberg, 2006). Both of these lead to coordination and harmonisation of structures and processes. In education this has meant the introduction of standards for teaching, curriculum, expected learning outcomes, school facilities, technologies and so on. Certain compatibility between schools and education systems is required for practical purposes. Standardising teaching and learning through fixed teaching schemes and predetermined learning outcomes is, however, the worst enemy of creativity. There are a number of examples how standardisation negatively affects schools and teaching (Sacks, 2000). When teachers teach by following externally set teaching standards and aim at narrow academic student achievement, they tend not to take risks, try new ways to teach and, thus, be more creative. A good example of an unexpected consequence of standardisation of teaching is diminishing role of collaboration in schools. Individualised testing as an element of standardisation puts personal performance before collective achievement is by definition reducing feeling of interdependency and care in schools. As Sawyer (2007) claims, collaboration is an important condition for creativity and ingenuity.

Barrier 3: Tougher test-based accountability The incentive-based educational reform movement has stimulated enormous debates between and within education and policymaking communities during the last two decades. Holding schools and teachers accountable for students' learning has become a fashionable global movement. Testing and measuring the performance of individuals (both students and teachers), schools, districts and nations have been boosted by the emergence of the educational accountability movement and international student assessments, such as the OECD PISA (Hargreaves & Shirley, 2009; Sahlberg, 2010). The key criterion in this accountability process is the test results determined by external standardised and often multiple-choice tests. According to the emerging evidence, this is leading to narrower curricula, more teacher-centred instruction, rote learning among students and even malpractice and corruption. Each of these, even alone, is damaging for trust, risk-taking and creativity in schools. A critical reviews of these can be found from Wayne Au (2008), Sharon Nichols and David Berliner (2007) and Peter Sacks (2000). School accountability is linked to consequences in the form of rewards such as higher teacher pay or promotion, or in the form of sanctions such as losing one's job or closing down a school. Interestingly, Barack Obama's administration is one of the strong advocates of merit-based pay in the United States. Private tutoring to improve student test scores and thus schools' performance is very common in Egypt, Japan, Korea, and many parts of eastern Europe, just to mention a few examples. Such consequences are certainly not the ways to promote creativity in classrooms. Should creativity be measured in schools? Based on how measurement in general affects teaching and learning the immediate response would be: 'Probably not.' Or at least this needs to be approached with caution. The process of human learning seems to follow much of the similar principles of measurement than measuring simultaneously momentum and place of a moving particle.

Heisenberg's uncertainty principle (1927) says that the measurement of position necessarily disturbs a particle's momentum, and vice versa. Application: the measurement of creativity necessarily disturbs a student's learning, and vice versa. At least we can conclude that the current culture of measuring students' academic achievements is greatly disturbing both teaching and learning.

The importance of fostering creativity in the classroom

Today's world is changing at an unprecedented rate — and for millions of educators around the world, now may be the single most critical period in history to embrace the benefits and importance of creativity in the classroom.

Looking back 10 years, no one could have predicted the sheer pace of change and the extraordinary circumstances that we'd be facing in today's world — from adapting to the learning needs in the wake of a global pandemic to empowering and building a digital generation capable of starting billion-dollar companies overnight; creativity and abstract thinking have become prerequisites in a student's repertoire of skills needed for the future of society. The last decade alone has seen entire industries completely transformed as a result of globalization and the digital revolution, access to technology and the potential for innovation has never been as accessible as it is today and educators in both physical, and now digital classrooms, play a vital role in fostering and encouraging this creativity.

What is creativity, really?

Creativity in itself is quite a broad subject. While it's easy to look at creativity as a particular skill and assume if you can draw or sing, you must be creative, the reality is far more nuanced. It's fair to say creativity has been the driving force behind the most groundbreaking innovations of our time. When you look around, we're surrounded by innovation that would not have happened were it not for incredibly creative and determined people embracing ambiguity, challenging the status quo, not taking no for an answer and discovering new ways to solve all kinds of problems.

We're living proof that it's nearly impossible to predict the advancements and technologies of tomorrow — from having instant access to the internet from the palm of our hands or having people all around the globe remain connected with a simple click of a button, love it or loathe it, the advancements we've made in technology affect almost everything we do today. It also influences most of our plans for the future, and yet what we take for granted today — TV streaming, GPS in our cars, libraries of content from all over the globe and online shopping — were not the norm, or so seamlessly integrated into our everyday life a decade ago.

The role and importance of creativity in the classroom

To find out more about the importance of nurturing creativity in the classroom, I spoke with Amber Kemp-Gerstel, a clinical child psychologist come modern day 'Art Attack', content creative and TV personality with more than a decade of experience in creative therapy. Our conversation shed some light on the role and importance of creativity in a classroom, with Amber explaining a classroom environment is one of the most important places to start encouraging and nurturing creativity in young people.

As adults, it can be easy to get caught up in the day-to-day and let the guardrails of society stunt our ability to think abstractly and pursue bold ideas that contradict the 'norm'. Conversely, children are best-positioned to develop their ways of thinking and solving problems as they are naturally inquisitive, open to learning, imaginative and they do not often feel embarrassed by novelty, since everything is new and consequently nothing is really abnormal. Generally speaking, with some teachers spending over 10,000 hours in a child's life as they progress from kinder to high school, it's crucial they nurture this behaviour and near limitless thinking, further support and encourage it as it plays an important role in developing the soft skills needed in life outside of the classroom.

In addition, the late Sir Ken Robinson was also vocal on the importance of interweaving creativity into the education system, stating education "takes us into a future we can't grasp", and thus creativity is imperative to overcoming blockers or challenges in the future.

Role of School in Fostering Creativity

1. Identification of Creative Children

The school management and teachers need to identify the children with creative instincts. A class consists of various kinds of learners such as gifted, average, quick and slow learners and creative children. It's chief responsibility of the teachers to recognise and acknowledge the creative works of children so that their creativity can be promoted and guided thoroughly. The teacher interacts with the class and spends most of the time with them so he can easily observe these creative children in his class.

2. Rewarding the Creative Achievements

Rewarding someone for doing something always stimulates and encourages him for doing something better next time. Reward is a source of extrinsic motivation that motivates the learners. When creative children are rewarded for their creative creations, they are energised to achieve another accomplishment through their creativity. Moreover, the process of rewarding creative learners for their accomplishments and achievements also motivates other students in the class. Reward is not only restricted to a sense of entitlement and symbolism rather it's a wonderful feeling that emerges and soothes the heart and soul of the learners.

3. Providing Condusive Environment

Creative children need occasions and opportunities to exhibit their creative potential and worth. School is the agency of formal education and a place where learners spend most of their time after home. School needs to organize certain activities, programs and competitions where learners get the opportunity to excel themselves and find the platform to exhibit their creativity before the audience and spectators. Therefore, in order to provide learners opportunity and promote creativity, school needs to provide condusive environment to the learners where they can display their creativity freely.

4. Providing Opportunities for Ego Involvement

School environment should provide opportunities to the learners that involve their ego rather than Id and superego. Involvement of ego promotes positive thinking, creates desire to learn something new and motivates the learners to be creative. They are encouraged to work in a team and learn various things from one another. It enables a learner to be focused and learning centric, fosters positive and healthy vibes and generates creative thinking.

5. Encouraging to Study Masterpieces

Class environment of the school should encourage learners to study Masterpieces of their areas of interests such as play, poetry, essays, articles, subject related textbooks and other relevant stuffs such as biographies, autobiographies, travelogues and fine pieces of literature. The artistic masterpieces and magnum Opus of the versatile authors foster creative genius and encourages to think out of the box. It also helps the learners to explore various aspects and dimensions of a subject.

6. Use of Special Teaching Techniques

Adopting special teaching techniques such as problem-solving, play way method, engaging learners in different activities and others harbour creativity in the learners. These techniques help the learners to use their mind and employ their potential and mind to accomplish the given tasks that shape their creative instincts and ideas.

7. Organisation of Co-Scholistic Activities

It has been observed that Co-Scholistic activities provide more opportunities to learners to express their creativity through various means and platforms. Scholastic activities are generally centred around the traditional way of teaching and learning but Co-Scholistic activities such as public speaking, performing in a play, singing, dancing, playing musical instruments and participating in debates, discussions and quizzes encourage the learners to excel and exhibit their potential among the audience.

8. Inculcating Self-Belief and Developing Self Confidence

Belief in self and confidence are the essential qualities to succeed in life. These attributes are a must for self development and achievement of your desired goal in life. The role and responsibilities of a school is to inculcate self esteem, belief and confidence in the learners and make them stronger to face real life challenges. Inculcating these virtues will lead the learners to be more creative, artistic and versatile.

9. Removal of Fear and Hesitation

There are many creative minds sitting silently in a classroom due to fear of being laughed at and hesitation. These learners may be bright, studious and creative but lack of confidence holds them back from expressing themselves. The school should create a learning environment condusive and favourable where learners could speak up their minds fearlessly and without any hesitation or confusion. The school should remove these barriers that occur in the way of exhibiting creativity.

10. Maintaining Discipline in the Class

Discipline is the key to success. A disciplined class always succeeds in achieving most of the aims and objectives. A proper discipline in the classroom helps in smooth learning and ensures thorough imparting of knowledge. A class that lacks discipline troubles everyone especially the creative learners who find it difficult to express their creativity due to indiscipline in the class. Hence, it's important for school and teachers to maintain proper discipline in the classroom so that creativity can be encouraged and promoted.

Conclusion

Creativity is the ability to think differently. It is a quality of an individual that is less ordinary. Creativity enables to think out of the box and construct wonder from waste. Some learners are born with this precious quality and some develop it through the experiences. Creativity is the foundation of innovation and inventions. Creative children are not only divergent thinkers but also unique creators. Most of the existing crisis can be resolved through creative approach. Creativity is the cherished virtue that separates the learners and provides a special identity. It eases the path of personal and social life of the learners. We need to identify and acknowledge such children who have creative instincts and the ability to think beyond. Their creativity should be recognised and promoted. Creativity is the solution to various complex issues and problems. It is the origin of innovation and invention. These innovations and inventions reduce the human efforts and enhance efficiency, utility and production. Therefore, it can be concluded that creativity resolves human issues and eases human efforts and optimises the outcomes. We need to foster creative instincts, temper and thinking in the learners from the beginning to help them use their full potential and skills.

Embracing creativity in the classroom is a great way to challenge the notion of static learning: the idea that there's merely one correct way to solve a problem or come to a solution. Whilst one plus one will always equal two, there are a multitude of ways to teach that concept. The advent of the internet and the omnipresence of connected devices has opened up new opportunities for people of all ages to have instant access to new information and different ways of thinking and doing things.

We know not everything always goes to plan the first time around, so it's critical to encourage young people to acknowledge this and find alternative and unique solutions to the challenges at hand, meanwhile building resilience and confidence in their ability.

All in all, creativity has become a prerequisite for innovation and will be an increasingly in-demand skill for jobs of the future. Creativity doesn't need to be a subject of its own, instead, it should be weaved into absolutely every aspect of learning and teaching.

CHAPTER FOURTEEN

KOHLBERG'S THEORY OF MORAL DEVELOPMENT:

Introduction:

Every day in the course of life, we determine wrong-pure, right-wrong, etc. under the shelter of logic. Today, the one who is considered to be great, may be put in the seat of the gods, and after a few days, he may be dragged down again by the counter-argument.Although such differences in principles and ideologies depend on various factors, the idea of good and evil is formed in people from childhood.Infact, as a child gets older, logical thinking develops and the sense of morality is created by relying on logical thinking. Like adults, children take on the sounds, lights, subjects, events around them in their own way, think, analyze and, above all, make decisions about them.Morality is a fundamental element of a child's social development. Children develop their morals and values by taking on family members or friends as 'Models'. Moreover, family traditions, religious education, etc. also help them to develop morals.

Our sense of right-wrong, good-evil is called moral sense. This moral feeling tends to change as the person grows older. Researchers at the university of chicago in the 1950s detailed Kohlberg's moral development. The primary source of his research was the psychologist Piaget's experiments on moral development. I have discussed kohlberg's theory of moral development.

Concept of Moral Behaviour:

Moral behavior is to behave in a way that is socially fixed or socially desirable. The word 'Moral' is derived from the latin word 'Mores' which means to follow certain rules and regulations. Moral behaviour is governed by moral concepts.And this moral concept is a combination of the behaviour that a particular society expects from all its members. In the course of life, a person gains experience in the need for a sense of principle and puts principles in front of him according to certain rules.Again according to many since morality is an acquired trait of the individual it is possible to develop and control it by education.Most educators believe in the latter belief and consider ethics as one of the goals of education.

Moral Development in Learners:

Kohlberg made some changes to the Piaget method. He wants to know the children's decision by highlighting the situation of two conflicting moral judgments. Based on the results of his experiments, he rearranged the stages of Piaget moral development and presented his own information. According to him, moral development depends on the development of wisdom and with the development of wisdom, children learn to judge the good and evil of the things around them, on the basis of which moral development begins.

Kohlberg (1927-87) submitted his dissertation on the moral development of children for a doctorate from the university of chicago, USA. His research reveals the futility of traditional theories on moral development. After teaching for 6 years at the university of chicago, he was invited to teach at Harvard university, where he spent his life researching on moral development.Kohlberg says there are three key elements in the moral development of an individual's life.

1) Cognitive Development: Kohlberg speaks of Piaget's policy of cognitive development as a condition of moral development. He says Piaget's proposed developmental level helps the individual make socially based moral judgments. That is, a person's moral judgment depends on his cognitive development. But Kohlberg also states that cognitive development is not the only condition or cause of moral development.

2) Moral Dilemma: Another element that helps in moral development is moral dilemma. Conflicting the external environment with conflicting thoughts or beliefs of the individual leads to cognitive conflict. The process of cognitive conflict is conducive to the creative or moral development of the individual.

3) Moral Reasoning or role taking ability: Whether a person will be able to put an end to his or her conflict depends on an element. Kohlberg calls this element the ability to take on roles. The ability to take on this role depends especially on his/her previous social experience and through it he/she gains additional social experience.

Lawrence Kohlberg, a psychologist belonging to the University of Harvard is known for putting forward a theory of the development of moral judgement in the individual, right from the years of early childhood. He has based his theory of moral development on the findings of his studies conducted on hundreds of children from different cultures.

He differs from the popular view that children imbibe the sense and methods of moral judgement from their parents and elders by way of learning. According to him as soon as we talk with children about morality, we find that they have many ways of making judgements which are not internalized from the outside, and which do not come in any direct and obvious way from parents, teachers and even peels, (Kohlberg, 1968). Going further he clarified that internal or cognitive processes like thinking and reasoning also play a major role in one's moral development, i.e. the way children make moral judgement depends on their level of intellectual development as well as on their upbringing and learning experiences.

Meaning & Concept of Morality:

The word moral comes from the Latin word 'Mors', which means custom or practice or a way of accomplishing things. Therefore it has come to mean 'belonging to manners and conduct of men' or 'pertaining to right and wrong, good in conduct'. Morality is the conformity to the moral code of social group. It is the internalization of a set of values, virtues, and ideas sanctioned by the society which becomes an integral part of the individual self through the process of development. It is considered a sum total of an individual's way of behaving which is judged in terms of ethical rightness or wrongness.

The term 'Morality' stands for following the moral code of society or conformity in behaviour to the manners, values and customs of the social group. It also includes a sense of right or wrong. Morality consists of ideals or rules that govern human conduct Morality has a, social reference. Moral standards vary from group to group depending upon what has been accepted by the group as the socially approved behaviour. True morality comes from within the individual. It is internal in nature and not imposed by external authority.

Hence the ability to make moral judgement plays an important facet of the total development of the child. Moral judgement involves the cognitive capacity and insight to see the relationship between the abstract principle and concrete cases and judge the situations as right or wrong, keeping in view the knowledge of moral standards.

The theory which most directly inspired the research on moral judgement has been that of Swiss psychologist, Jean Piaget (1928, 1932) who endeavoured to interpret the child's concept of moral rules. He attempted to test children's moral judgement towards intentional and unintentional wrong-doing and described six types of moral thoughts which appeared in children of different age groups. More recently, studies on moral judgement have been conducted by Kohlberg (1968), in which he asked the children to judge the morality of conduct as described in the stories.

Different Educational Commissions and committees in our country have expressed their deep concern over the declining values in human activities and emphasized on providing value oriented education. The National Policy on Education-1986 has categorically stated "The growing concern over erosion of essential values has brought to focus the need for readjustment in the curriculum in order to make education a forceful tool for the cultivation of moral and social values". The Education Commission of 1964-66 has noted, "A serious defect in the school curriculum is the absence of provision for education in social, moral and spiritual values. In the life of the majority of Indians, religion is a great motivating force and is intimately bound up with the formation of character and inculcation of ethical values. A national system of education related to life needs and aspirations of the people cannot afford to ignore this purposeful force". Thus concerns are being expressed to inculcate right moral values in our present generation.

Meaning of Moral Development: Hemming in his book, "The Development of Children's Moral Values' writes, "Moral development is the process in which the child acquires the values esteemed by his community, acquires a sense of right and wrong in terms of these values, learns to regulate his personal desires and compulsions so that, when a situational conflict arises, he does, what he ought to do rather than what he wants to do. Moral development is the process by which a community seeks to transfer the egocentricity of the baby into the social behaviour of the mature adult."

Moral development includes moral behaviour and moral concepts:

1. **Moral behaviour:** Moral behaviour means behaviour in conformity with the moral code of the social group. The term 'Moral' comes from the Latin word 'mores' meaning manners, customs and folkways. Moral behaviour not only conforms to social standards but also it is carried out voluntarily. It is always accompanied by a feeling of responsibility for one's acts. It involves giving primary consideration to tile welfare of l he group and considering personal gain or desires as having secondary importance.

2. **Moral concepts:** Moral concepts arc the rules of' behaviour to which the members of a culture become accustomed and which determine the expected behaviour patterns of all group members.

3.2 Meaning of Moral Judgment: Moral judgments are evaluations or opinions formed as to whether some action or inaction, intention, motive, character trait, or a person as a whole is (more or less) good or bad as measured against some standard of Good. The moral judgments of actions (or inaction) are usually the primary focus of any discussion of Moral Judgments in particular and Ethical analysis in general. This is because the judgments of intentions, character traits, and persons are generally based on the judgment of actions that the intention, motive, character trait, or person might potentially do or not do.

What distinguishes moral judgments from non moral judgments is the context of the statement. Philosophy, and particularly Ethics, differs from the sciences in one very important way. All of the sciences, both 'hard' and "Soft', deal with descriptions of Reality. They purport to describe in varying levels of detail, what **is** about Reality. Ethics, on the other hand, is that branch of Philosophy that describes what one **ought**. All of the various philosophers, in all of their various works on Ethics, are detailing what you "Should" do or how things "Should" be, not what is. In answer to the questions "What should I do?" or "What is the 'right' thing to do?", ethics answers "You should do what you 'ought' to!" So moral judgments are judgments about what one "ought" to do (or not do), or have done (or not done).

Types of Moral Judgement:

We can group moral judgments into two broad classes. There are "before-the-fact" moral judgments, and there are "after-the-fact" moral judgments. Before-the-fact judgments are those made before the action (or inaction) takes place. They are made based on the best information available at the time as to what the moral landscape holds and what its future shape will be. These are judgments about what you "ought to do (or not do) and whether what you are planning to do (or not do) is Good or Bad. After-the-fact moral judgments are made after the action (or inaction) has taken place, and are based on 20/20 hindsight view of the actual consequences. These are judgments about what you "ought to have done (or not done)", and whether your actual actions were Good or Bad.

A second major distinction of moral judgments is that they can only be made of an agent with the freedom or will to choose. Moral judgments are judgments of certain choices, or potential choices, where the one who chooses is aware that there is a choice, and has the capability to choose. A person who cannot do other than what was done, is not subject to moral judgment. But if a person has the freedom to choose alternatives, then that person's intentional, or unintentional actions or inaction can be subject to moral judgments. This argument is the ethical basis of the "Insanity" defence. The insanity defence argues that the accused cannot be considered guilty because the accused was unable to make a choice of an alternate behaviour. The behaviour exhibited was "unavoidable". This line of reasoning is never too successful when it is applied to the average human, with an average degree of intelligence. But it is the reason we do not make moral judgments about what a falling tree does on its way down. If the tree happens to kill someone, we don't judge that the tree "ought not to have done that" because the tree had no other alternative.

The third important distinction is knowledge. In order to be able to make a choice, we have to be aware that there are alternatives. If our knowledge about our current situation is thin, or our knowledge about how reality behaves is thin, then we might come to the conclusion that there are no better alternatives. We might make a choice that we believe is the correct one, but because our knowledge is thin, we overlook a better one. In such a case, we could make an after-the-fact judgment about what we ought to have done, if we had had better information, but any before-the-fact moral judgment we might make about what we did, has to be based on the knowledge available to us at that time.

Theories of Moral Development: Moral development is one of the most significant aspects of the personality development. It is a major task of society and education. Moral development proceeds along with social development. A person whose social development has been disturbed due to some, or the other reason, a person who is socially maladjusted develops immoral behaviour.

Immoral behaviour is that behaviour which fails to conform to social expectations. Such behaviour arises not due to ignorance of social aspect ions, but due to intentional disapproval of social standards or lack of feelings of obligation to conform. Similarly a person who has been deprived of opportunity to learn social standards or lack of feelings of obligation to conform. Similarly a person who has been deprived of the opportunity to learn social behaviour develops unmoral or non-moral behaviour. Unmoral or non moral behaviour arises due to ignorance of what the social group expects rather than intentional violation of the group's standards.

Stages of Moral Development:

For studying the process of moral development in human beings, Kohlberg first defined moral development as the development of an individual's sense of justice. For estimating one's sense of justice he concentrated on one's views on morality with the help of a test of moral judgement consisting of a set of moral dilemmas. For instance, should a man who cannot afford the medicine his dying wife needs, steal it? Should a doctor mercy-kill a fatally ill person suffering terrible pain? Is it better to save the life of one important person or a lot of unimportant persons? With the help of the responses he got from his subjects he came to the conclusion that like the Piagetial stages of cognitive development, there also exist universal stages in the development of moral values, and the movement from one stage to another depends on cognitive abilities rather than the simple acquisition of moral values of one's parents, elders and peers. He then identified three levels of moral development, each containing two stages as shown in the following table:

Table: Kohlberg's Six Stages of Moral Development

Table: Kohlberg's Six Stages of Moral Development

Level I	Pre-moral (Age 4 to 10 years)
Stage 1 :	The stage of obedience for avoiding punishment
Stage 2 :	The stage of conforming to obtain rewards and favours in return
Level II	Conventional morality (Age 10 to 13 years)
Stage 3 :	The stage of maintaining mutual relations and approval of others
Stage 4 :	The stage of obedience for avoiding censure by higher authority or social systems
Level III	Self accepted moral principles (Age 13 or not until middle or later adulthood or never)
Stage 5:	Stage of conforming to the democratically accepted law and mores of community welfare
Stage 6:	Stage of conforming to the universal ethical principles and the call of one's conscience

id.pinterest.com

Let us now briefly discuss these levels and stages of morality.

Pre-moral level (4 to 10 years). The child begins to make judgements about what is right or wrong, good or bad. However, the standards by which he measures the morality are those of others. He is persuaded to take such judgement either to avoid punishment or to earn rewards. Development of morality at this level usually follows the following two stages:

Stage 1: In the beginning, the child's morality is controlled by the fear of punishment. He tries to obey his parents and elders purely to avoid reproof and punishment.

Stage 2; In the second stage of the pre-moral level, children's moral judgement is based on self-interest and considerations of what others can do for them in return. Here they value a thing because it has some practical utility for them. They obey the orders of their parents and elders and abide by some rules and regulations, because it serves their interests.

Conventional morality level (10 to 13 years). At this stage also, children's moral Judgement is controlled by the likes and dislikes of others-the conventions, rules and regulations and the law and order system maintained within society. Stealing or mercy-killing would thus be judged wrong because it is considered wrong by society at large and by the legal system. In this way, the conventional level of morality may be regarded as the level where the child identifies with authority. **It is characterized by the following two stages:**

Stage 3: In the early years of the second level of moral development, the child's moral judgement is based on the desire to obtain approval of others and avoid being disliked by being declared a good boy or a good girl. For this purpose he begins to judge the intentions and likes or dislikes of others and acts accordingly.

Stage 4: In the later years of the conventional morality level, children's moral judgements are governed by conventions as well as the laws and mores of the social system. The standards of others are now so established that it becomes a convention to follow them. The children now follow the rules and regulations of society and take decisions about things being right or wrong with a view to avoiding censure by the elders, authorities or the social system.

Self-accepted moral principles level (Age 13 or during late adulthood). This marks the highest level of attainment of true morality as the controlling force for making moral judgements now rests with the individual himself. He does not value a thing or conform to an idea merely because of consideration of the views of others, conventions or the law and order system of society but because it fits into the framework of his self-accepted moral principles. This level is also characterized by two separate stages:

Stage 5: At this stage the individual's moral judgements are internalized in such a form that he responds positively to authority only if he agrees with the principles upon which the demands of authority are based. The individual at this stage begins to think in rational terms, valuing the rights of human beings and the welfare of society. For example, at this stage in deference to the rights of the human being, the decision about mercy-killing may be left to the individual who is suffering, and if so needed, the concerned laws may be amended for the welfare of society at large.

Stage 6: At this stage, the controlling forces for making moral judgements are highly internalized. The decisions of the individual are now based upon his conscience and the belief in universal principles of respect, justice and equality. He does what he, as an individual thinks right regardless of legal restrictions or the opinion of others. Thus, at this stage people act according to the inner voice of their conscience and lead a life that they can without self-condemnation or feeling of guilt or shame.

Kohlberg chose a few features of human nature as the basis of his doctrine. The features are as follows:

A) He originally tried to explain the process of moral development, so he did not specifically mention the development of childhood, but he did admit that in childhood, a person has some cognitive development.As a result of this development he /she can distinguish between the material environment and the human environment or the social environment. The main feature of the human environment is where interactions take place, this interaction is the basis of moral development.

B) Kohlberg says there is no provocative center of moral conduct. By Conscience he means justice or fairness. Therefore, for him, the sense of conscience is rational, that is, according to him, moral development is a kind of cognitive development.

C) Kohlberg says of human nature that they can distinguish between their own manifest behaviour, intention of behaviour, and the intrinsic effect of this behaviour.These three powers of man, according to Kohlberg, contribute to his moral development.

Kohlberg's model of Moral Development:

In one of his essays, published in 1984, Kohlberg divided people into two groups in terms of moral development. These are discussed below:

1) A type: Kohlberg says that the influence of authority and rules on moral development can be noticed in some individuals. These individuals do not perform moral behaviour very spontaneously. These people are classified as A.

2) B type: There are some people who manage their own moral behaviour in terms of an improved way of life. Among them is the spontaneity of moral conduct. They are classified as B

Kohlberg says that in moral development there is a tendency for class A people to be promoted to class B, but there is no tendency for class B people to be class A. In most cases, however, individuals try to maintain their own class characteristics during moral development.

Significance of Moral Development in Education:

The application of kohlberg's theory in the field of education is extremely important for the benefit of both the individual and society. Kohlberg himself has taken moral development seriously in education and has discussed strategies for moral development.According to kohlberg, the most important aspect of moral development is moral conflict. So the teacher will raise the issue of moral conflict in the classroom as much as possible.

The teacher can take the following steps in this regard

1) The difference in the intellectual meaning of the students in the classroom is conducive to the onset of moral conflict. That is why teachers and students should be informed about their intellectual value.

2) The classroom environment will be one where students can openly discuss ethical conflicts. The teacher can exercise his authority as required in making any decision regarding the lower moral conflict. However, the teacher will ensure that the older students in the upper class end the moral conflict through mutual discussion and exchange of trust.

3) Confidence in students and their opinions need to be taken seriously. Ethical education is more effective by teachers who are dear to the students and who have a sweet relationship with the students.

4) It is not easy to build trust between students and sweet student-teacher relationship. Enough time is needed to be aware of the individual teacher's assessment and how he or she will treat the student. It takes time for the teacher to see how sensitive the situation is and to see if the student's thoughts are normal.The teacher will be aware of this and after gaining the necessary experience, he will take appropriate measures to implement the ethics.

5) Teachers will be sensitive about students' attitudes. If a student is emotionally traumatized during a discussion on moral conflict, the teacher will discuss and advise him / her separately. The teacher will encourage the student to express himself freely.

Kohlberg chose a few features of human nature as the basis of his doctrine. The features are as follows:

A) He originally tried to explain the process of moral development, so he did not specifically mention the development of childhood, but he did admit that in childhood, a person has some cognitive development.As a result of this development he /she can distinguish between the material environment and the human environment or the social environment. The main feature of the human environment is where interactions take place, this interaction is the basis of moral development.

B) Kohlberg says there is no provocative center of moral conduct. By Conscience he means justice or fairness. Therefore, for him, the sense of conscience is rational, that is, according to him, moral development is a kind of cognitive development.

C) Kohlberg says of human nature that they can distinguish between their own manifest behaviour, intention of behaviour, and the intrinsic effect of this behaviour.These three powers of man, according to Kohlberg, contribute to his moral development.

Kohlberg's model of Moral Development:

In one of his essays, published in 1984, Kohlberg divided people into two groups in terms of moral development. These are discussed below:

1) A type: Kohlberg says that the influence of authority and rules on moral development can be noticed in some individuals. These individuals do not perform moral behaviour very spontaneously. These people are classified as A.

2) B type: There are some people who manage their own moral behaviour in terms of an improved way of life. Among them is the spontaneity of moral conduct. They are classified as B

Kohlberg says that in moral development there is a tendency for class A people to be promoted to class B, but there is no tendency for class B people to be class A. In most cases, however, individuals try to maintain their own class characteristics during moral development.

Significance of Moral Development in Education:

The application of kohlberg's theory in the field of education is extremely important for the benefit of both the individual and society. Kohlberg himself has taken moral development seriously in education and has discussed strategies for moral development.According to kohlberg, the most important aspect of moral development is moral conflict. So the teacher will raise the issue of moral conflict in the classroom as much as possible.

The teacher can take the following steps in this regard

1) The difference in the intellectual meaning of the students in the classroom is conducive to the onset of moral conflict. That is why teachers and students should be informed about their intellectual value.

2) The classroom environment will be one where students can openly discuss ethical conflicts. The teacher can exercise his authority as required in making any decision regarding the lower moral conflict. However, the teacher will ensure that the older students in the upper class end the moral conflict through mutual discussion and exchange of trust.

3) Confidence in students and their opinions need to be taken seriously. Ethical education is more effective by teachers who are dear to the students and who have a sweet relationship with the students.

4) It is not easy to build trust between students and sweet student-teacher relationship. Enough time is needed to be aware of the individual teacher's assessment and how he or she will treat the student. It takes time for the teacher to see how sensitive the situation is and to see if the student's thoughts are normal.The teacher will be aware of this and after gaining the necessary experience, he will take appropriate measures to implement the ethics.

5) Teachers will be sensitive about students' attitudes. If a student is emotionally traumatized during a discussion on moral conflict, the teacher will discuss and advise him / her separately. The teacher will encourage the student to express himself freely.

Conclusion:

From the above discussion of the stages of moral development, it is clear that although children begin to think about morality in terms of justice or right and wrong at a very early age, yet they have to wait until adolescence or adulthood for the dawning of the stage of true morality. Also, it is not essential that all people pass through the third level of moral development. Most adults are not able to cross the second level and few can reach stage 5, and among these there are very few who, being intellectually quite sound, can think rationally and base their moral judgement purely on the dictates of their conscience at the risk of life and property.

CHAPTER FIFTEEN

BEHAVIOURISM, AN APPROACH TO LEARNING IN CLASSROOM

Introduction:

Behaviourism is a theory of learning which states that all behaviours are developed through the interaction with the environment, also known as conditioning. It is also described Behavioural Psychology. Two factors are mostly involved in this theory i.e. Stimulus and Response.

In behaviourist's view, Behaviours can be created or changed through only the exposure of specific stimuli, no or less genetic or hereditary factor are involved in this mechanism.

There is no fundamental differences between human and animal behaviour. Therefore, different experiments can be carried out on animals as well as humans (i.e., Comparative Psychology).

Consequently, small animals like rats and pigeons became the popular choice of experiment for behaviourists, as their environments and stimuli could be easily controlled. From the experiments the studies can be made in a systematic and observable manner.

The behaviourist movement began in 1913 when John Watson wrote an article entitled 'Psychology as the behaviourist views it,' which set out a number of underlying assumptions regarding methodology and behavioural analysis.

Behaviourists believe that psychology should focus on measurable and observable physical behaviours and how these behaviours can be manipulated by changes in the external environment. ... The four main psychologists who lead to the **development of behaviourist** theory were **Pavlov, Watson, Thorndike**, and **Skinner.**

Here in this article, we will discuss about the types of behaviourism, different experiments and the significance of behaviourism in learning at school.

Types of behaviourism:
1. Classical Conditioning (By Pavlov)
2. Modern Classical Conditioning (By Watson)
3.Operant Conditioning (By Skinner and Thorndike)

- **1. Pavlov and His Experiments:**

Pavlov contributed to many areas of physiology and neurological sciences. Most of his work and researches are involving the facts of conditioning and involuntary reflex actions. But the most famous one is the experiment of classical conditioning with dogs, who salivated in response to a bell tone. Pavlov showed that when a bell was rang each time the dog was fed, the dog learned to associate the sound with the presentation of the food, is another example of behaviourism.

Pavlov's Experiment on Classical Conditioning Theory:
The best-known and most thorough early work on classical conditioning was done by Ivan Pavlov. During his research on the physiology of digestion in dogs, Pavlov developed a procedure that enabled him to study the digestive processes of animals over long periods of time. He redirected the animal's digestive fluids outside the body, where they could be measured. Pavlov noticed that his dogs began to salivate in the presence of the technician who normally fed them, rather than simply salivating in the presence of food. Pavlov called the dogs' anticipatory salivation "psychic secretion". Putting these informal observations to an experimental test, Pavlov presented a stimulus, bell and then gave the dog food; after a few repetitions, the dogs started to salivate in response to the food in association with bell. After that one day he only rang the bell but did not give the food the dog but still the dog salivate. Pavlov concluded that if a particular stimulus in the dog's surroundings was present when the dog was given food then that stimulus could become associated with food and cause

salivation on its own.

Classical Conditioning:

Here,

1.Food is the Unconditioned Stimulus (US). This means that the food causes the response of salivation without previous learning.

2.Bell is the Conditioned Stimulus (CS). This is the stimulus which is paried with the food to make the dog eventually salivate to just the sound of the bell alone.

3.Salivation is initially the Unconditioned Response (UR) when paired with the food (US), and eventually becomes the Conditioned Response (CR) when paired with the bell.

- **2. J. B. Watson and His Experiments:**

John Broadus Watson, an American psychologist who codified and publicized behaviourism, an approach to psychology that, in his view, was restricted to the objective, experimental study of the relations between environment and human behaviour. Watsonian behaviourism became the dominant psychology in the United States during the 1920s and 1930s.Watson received a Ph.D. in Psychology from the University of Chicago (1903), where he then taught. He established a laboratory for research in comparative, or animal, psychology. He articulated his first statements on behaviourist psychology in the article titled "Psychology as a Behaviourist Views It" (1913), claiming that psychology is the science of human behaviour which is similar to animal behaviour, should be studied under exacting laboratory conditions. His first major work, "Behaviour: An Introduction to Comparative Psychology, 1914" where he promoted conditioned responses as the ideal experimental tool. In 1918 Watson ventured into the relatively unexplored field of infant study. In one of his classic experiments and one of the most controversial in the history of psychology—he conditioned love to fear of white rats and other furry objects in "Little Albert," an orphaned 9 month-old boy.

Little Albert Experiment:

The Little Albert experiment was a famous psychology experiment conducted by John B. Watson and his graduate student, Rosalie Rayner. Previously, Russian physiologist Ivan Pavlov had conducted experiments demonstrating the conditioning process in dogs. Watson took Pavlov's research a step further by showing that emotional reactions could be classically conditioned in people.The participant in the experiment was a 9 month old child Albert. Albert liked white rats very much. Watson and Rayner exposed him to a series of stimuli including a white rat, a rabbit, a monkey, masks, and burning newspapers and observed the boy's reactions. The boy initially showed no fear of any of the objects. But from the next time, when Albert was exposed to the rat, Watson made a loud noise by hitting a metal pipe with a hammer. As a result, the child began to cry after hearing the loud noise. After repeatedly exposure of the white rat with the loud noise, Albert began to expect a loud noise associated with the white rat. Soon, it affected the mind of Albert and he started to cry after seeing the white rat.

Watson and Rayner wrote: *"The instant the rat was shown, the baby began to cry. Almost instantly he turned sharply to the left, fell over on [his] left side, raised himself on all fours and began to crawl away so rapidly that he was caught with difficulty before reaching the edge of the table."*

Modern Classical Conditioning:

The Little Albert experiment is a perfect example of how classical conditioning can be done. From this we can successively introduce to some important terms.

1. Neutral Stimulus: It is the stimulus that does not primarily create a response (Here the white rat).

2. Unconditioned Stimulus: A stimulus that generates a reflexive response (Here the loud noise).

3. Unconditioned Response: A natural reaction to the given stimulus (Here it is the fear of white rat).

4. Conditioned Stimulus: A stimulus that synthesize a response after repeatedly being paired with an unconditioned stimulus (Here the white rat).

5. Conditioned Response: The response caused by the conditioned stimulus (Here it is the fear).

After conditioning, Albert feared not just the white rat, but a wide variety of similar white objects. His fear included other furry objects including Raynor's fur coat and Watson wearing a Santa Claus beard.

- **3. Thorndike and His Experiment:**

Edward Thorndike (1898) is famous in psychology for his work on learning theory that lead to the development of operant conditioning within Behaviourism.

Cat and Puzzle box Experiment:

Thorndike's most famous experiment was with the cat placed in a puzzle box. The hungry cat was put in the puzzle box and a fish, as an incentive, was put out-side the cage a little beyond its reach. The box was designed in such a way that the door of the cage can be released by some simple act like depressing a lever inside the cage.

At first, the cat made a varied attempts to reach the food in a trial and error process such as jumping up and down, clawing at the bars, scratching the cage, whaling around trying to push the bars, pawing and shaking movable parts of the cage etc., but all attempts proved to vain.

Ultimately by chance her paw fell on the loop of the rope and the door opened. The cat jumped out immediately and ate the fish. Next day, the cat was put in the box again, this time she took less time in coming out and in the subsequent trials the time decreased further so much so that the stage reached when the cat came out soon after being put inside by directly striking the latch with her paw without any random movement. This is how she learnt to reach its goal.

The Law of Effect Principle :

Edward Thorndike suggested that:"Responses that produce a satisfying effect in a particular situation become more likely to occur again in that situation, and responses that produce a discomforting effect become less likely to occur again in that situation (Gray, 2011, p. 108–109)."

- **B. F. Skinner and His Experiments:**

B.F. Skinner proposed his theory on operant conditioning by conducting various experiments on animals. He used a special box known

as "Skinner Box" for his experiment on rats.

Skinner Box:

a)First experiment:

In his first experiment, he placed a hungry rat inside the Skinner box. The rat was initially inactive inside the box, but gradually as it began to explore around. While exploring, the rat discovered a lever, upon pressing which; food was released inside the box. After it filled its hunger, it started exploring the box again, and after a while it pressed the lever for the second time as it grew hungry again. This phenomenon continued for the third, fourth and the fifth time, and after a while, the hungry rat immediately pressed the lever once it was placed in the box. Then the conditioning was deemed to be complete.

Here, the action of pressing the lever is an operant response/behaviour, and the food released inside the chamber is the reward. The experiment is also known as Instrumental Conditioning Learning as the response is instrumental in getting food.

b) Second Experiment:

In his second experiment, Skinner placed a rat in a chamber in the similar manner, but instead of keeping it hungry, he subjected the chamber to an unpleasant electric current. The rat having experienced the discomfort started to desperately move around the box and accidentally knocked the lever. Pressing of the lever immediately seized the flow of unpleasant current. After a few times, the rat had smartened enough to go directly to the lever in order to prevent itself from the discomfort.

Theory of Reinforcement by Skinner:

His first experiment deals with the effects of positive reinforcement. Upon pressing the lever, the hungry rat was served with food, which filled its hunger; hence, it's a positive reinforcement.

In second experiment, the electric current reacted as the negative reinforcement, and the consequence of escaping the electric current made sure that the rat repeated the action again and again. Here too, the pressing of the lever is an operant response, and the complete stop of the electric current flow is its reward.

Skinner emphasizes the importance of behaviourism specifically its procedures in a classroom setting. One might briefly describe a procedure of a behaviour modification as follows:

1.Favourable environment by removing unfavourable stimuli in complicate learning should be helpful.

2.Role of choosing the proper reinforcers for desired behavioural manifestations is important

3.Once a pattern of desired behaviours has begun, slacken off the number of times reinforcers also effective.

Significance of Behaviourism in learning in classroom:

1.During teaching process teachers should use perfect stimulus which can enhance the student's learning ability.

2. Teacher can avoid those stimulus which will produce negative effects in students.

3. Excessive punishments are harmful for students.

4. Some words of appreciation like good, very good, are overall helps in the student's performance.

But if these are used in daily tasks, then students become over confident, which isnot good for them.

5. For long time memory, more practises should be carried out after learning.

6. It helps to increase desirable behaviours of students and decrease the undesirable behaviours also.

7. It is the responsibility of teacher to choose effective reinforcers and make timely exposure of that.

Conclusion:

Behaviourism has made a major contribution to education in the area of teaching method. According to Driscoll (2000:16), one major contribution of behaviourism to education is use of the 'Drill and Practise methodology ' during instructional process. Here teacher present a stimulus to the learners in form of words inscribed in black board and students are instructed to read them loudly (response). The intension is to make the word sink in their minds effectively. This method is very effective in language learning.

The central belief of a behaviourist is that students learn through reinforcement - Constant feedback that tells them whether what they are doing is right or wrong. This comes in the form of test scores, homework marks and more.

So, basically in this way a teacher can conditioned the behaviour of students by introducing different stimulus. Lastly we only can say the core meaning by the words of Watson that, "Give me a dozen healthy infants, well-formed, and my own specified world to bring them up in and I'll guarantee to take any one at random and train him to become any type of specialist I might select–doctor, lawyer, artist–regardless of his talents, penchants, tendencies, abilities, vocations and race of his ancestors" (p. 104).

CHAPTER SIXTEEN

BEHAVIOURAL PROBLEMS OF ADOLESCENTS

Introduction:

Adolescence is the period of life when a child develops into an adult. An adult meansthe period from puberty to maturity terminating legally at the age of majority. In other words , Adolescence is the period of changeover or transition (a change from one state or form to another) between childhood to adulthood.

During this period of transition, many changes were observed in adolescents. Many of them are good as well as some of them are bad. Generally, Behavioral problems begin during childhood to adolescents. It is also a time of growth and maturation in the brain. It is a time when many new behaviours begin to emerge, some of them are good and some of them are bad. Adolescence is often associated with Behavioral problems. Adolescence is the period of all round development of a child. Mental and Behavioralchanges of a child also took place in this period.

Behavioural problems of adolescents is a common concern for their parents. Behavioural problems means uncertain changes comes in the behaviour of a person. Adolescence, the transitional phase of growth development between childhood and adulthood.

The World Health Organization (WHO) defines an adolescent as any person between ages 10 and 19. This age range falls within WHO's definition of *young people*, which refers to individuals between ages 10 and 24. In many societies, however, adolescence is narrowly equated with puberty and the cycle of physical changes culminating in reproductive maturity. In other societies adolescence is understood in broader terms that encompass psychological, social, and moral terrain as well as the strictly physical aspects of maturation. In these societies the term *adolescence* typically refers to the period between ages 12 and 20 and is roughly equivalent to the word *teens*.

What Does Behavioural Problem Mean?

Behavioural problems are those that aren't considered typically acceptable. Nearly everyone can have a moment of disruptive behaviour or an error in judgment. However, behaviour problem is a consistent pattern. Behaviourproblem can vary in terms of severity. They can occur in children as well as in adults. There are many symptoms to know about these problems, if your children have following qualities:

- **abuse of alcohol**
- **agitation**
- **angry, defiant behaviour**
- **carelessness**
- **disinterest or withdrawal from daily life**
- **drug use**
- **emotional flatness**
- **excessive, disruptive talking**
- **hoarding useless objects**
- **inappropriate behaviour**
- **inflated self-esteem or overconfidence**
- **obsessive thoughts**
- **poor judgment**
- **property damage**
- **self-injury**

Behavioural problems can range from the absence of emotions to aggressive emotions.

Causes of BehaviouralProblem:

- **Identity**
  Young people are busy working out who they are and where they fit

in the world. You might notice your child trying out new things like clothing styles, music, art or friendship groups. Friends, family, media, culture and more shape your child's choices in these years.

- **Independence**
Your child will probably want more independence about things like how he gets to places, how he spends his time, who he spends time with, and what he spends money on. As your child becomes more independent, it'll probably mean some changes in your family routines and relationships, as well as your child's friendships.

- **Responsibility**
Your child might be keen to take on more responsibility both at home and at school. This could include things like cooking dinner once a week or being on the school council.

- **New experiences**
Your child is likely to look for new experiences, including risky experiences. This is normal as your child explores her own limits and abilities, as well as the boundaries you set. She also needs to express herself as an individual.

But because of how teenage brains develop, your child might sometimes struggle with thinking through consequences and risks before he tries something new.

- **Values**
This is the time your child starts to develop a stronger individual set of values and morals. She'll question more things, and she's also learning that she's responsible for her own actions, decisions and consequences. Your words and actions help shape your child's sense of 'right' and 'wrong'.

- **Influences**
Your child's friends and peers might influence your child, particularly his behaviour, appearance, interests, sense of self and self-esteem. You still have a big influence on long-term things like your child's career choices, values and morals.

- **Sexual identity**
Your child might start to have romantic relationships or go on 'dates'. But these aren't always intimate relationships. For some young people, intimate or sexual relationships don't occur until later on in life.

- **Media**
  The internet, mobile phones and social media can influence how your child communicates with friends and learns about the world.

- **Decision-making**
  Your child might go through a stage where he seems to act without thinking a lot of the time. Your child's decision-making skills are still developing, and he's still learning that actions have consequences and even risks sometimes.

- **Moods and feelings**
  Your child might show strong feelings and intense emotions, and her moods might seem unpredictable. These emotional ups and downs can lead to increased conflict. They happen partly because your child's brain is still learning how to control and express emotions in a grown-up way.

- **Sensitivity to others**
  As your child gets older, he'll get better at reading and understanding other people's emotions. But while your child is developing these skills, he can sometimes misread facial expressions or body language.

- **Self-consciousness**
  Teenage self-esteem is often affected by appearance – or by how teenagers think they look. As your child develops, she might feel self-conscious about her physical appearance. She might also compare her body with those of friends and peers.

CONCLUSION:

The behavioural problems in children are common. They are always often under-recognised. Improved recognition demands that a good assessment is being carried out and a heightened index of suspicion for the common behavioural problems.

It's normal for parents to worry that their child with disability won't make friends easily or be accepted into a peer group. It helps to remember that the rate of social and emotional development varies widely for young people.

Teens who miss a lot of school because of a physical or mental illness, or who have a visible physical disability, might find it harder to make and keep friendships. This doesn't mean that friendships won't happen. There might be other ways for your child to form friendships, such as joining community groups and online networks. Give your child lots of love and support at home. Boost confidence and self-esteem by focusing on your child's strengths and interests.

149

CHAPTER SEVENTEEN

ADOLESCENT-CONFUSED BETWEEN FEELINGS AND NORMS.

Introduction:

Developmental psychology says adolescence as a 'transitional phase'. Adolescents want freedom where society expects them to follow the rules and norms. Adolescence is the stage where adolescents need autonomy. They try to be independent, try to act independently, and try to think independently. They want their freedom from anything by any means-breaking rules, challenging authorities or sometimes by questioning parents and others too. In this stage the adolescents are mentally and physically adult, but society and its norms make them more topsy-turvy. Adolescence acts as bridge in-between childhood and adulthood. In another point of view it is the stage from where puberty or sexual maturity takes place and it continues until the physical growth becomes complete. Adolescents are actually taking the first step from carefree childhood to complex responsibility of adulthood. G.Stanly Hall termed this stage as "Storm and Stress" (Hall, 1904)

The Adolescence stage is taking place from puberty to around age 18or 19. Puberty is typically starts between 11 to 13. Different physical changes happen in this stage mainly menstruation in the female and production of sperm in the male. So at this stage how adolescent will deal with these problems like unfamiliar body changes that is strange as well to them, attraction and making relationship with opposite sex members and different emotional changes that ultimately lead different behavioral changes in

150

them. "Adolescents with behavior problems are at risk for numerous problems in the academic, social and daily functioning" (Loeber& Farrington, 1999)

From the society point of view problem behaviors are those that are not socially desirable, those are against the societal norms. According to O'Brien (2003)," problem behavior is an act of a person who either forms significant risk to the health and/or safety to oneself or others or who "exerts momentous negative impact on his/her own quality of life or the quality of life of others."

Behavioral problems of adolescents:

Adolescents generally engage in such behavior under pressure of peer groups. Peer groups play an important role in their life. Peer group not always act as a negative influence, sometimes it can be positive, encouraging and supportive too. But Maximum behavioral problem that adolescents adopt, come from his peer group. Often, adolescents do risky inappropriate behavior under peer pressure because they want to fit in it and they do not want to be left out.

Substances like use of drugs or alcohol skip class, failure in school etc they learn from their peer groups. They cannot fulfill the expectation of parents and academic too. They become slow learners and very often problem learners. They also fail to meet own expectation and ultimately become depressed about their own life they start to think that nothing is going to his or her own way. It also causes the problem of day dreaming. As they fail to fulfill expectations they started to meet it by day dreaming only. Start to spend more and more time by himself in his room and here low self esteem is also included. These maladaptive practices (daydreaming) become a psychological problem for them and also cause different behavioural problem because they cannot adjust with his environment also. In this stage adolescents always want do experiments about their limitations without knowing the consequences, it lead them to do different problematic behaviour. They try to do different things which are different from others, that make them unique and for it without proper information they can involved in risks.

Behaviorally adolescent first face the problem with the complexities of sudden changes in the roles. A boy who used to play with his female friend from his childhood, suddenly he is forbidden to do so. This is the first experience an adolescent face during this stage. Before understanding the changes they are forced to do so. Therefore they try to do much risky behaviours and not to follow these rules.

Violence during adolescence is a common behavioural problem in adolescents. According to WHO," It causes nearly a third of all adolescent male deaths in low- and middle-income countries in the WHO Region of the Americas." They are trying to be independent, their act is done and judged by their own code, own rules. They don't want to follow the societal rules and parents. At that time they are actually out of control from their parents. Sexual violence also affects adolescents. So here parents playing an important role, they control important resources. If they treat their adolescents in a more friendly way without imposing rules and control over them, then the adolescents will less likely to join any risky behavior.

They feel they are adult enough to take decisions by own, they always to things by depending on the rules and codes they have set for them. They think they do not need authority any more they become risk taker and try to explore new things that sometimes may become dangerous from them and it is one of the major behavioural problems of adolescent. Their risk taking behavior always cause stress for their parent.

The major influence of adolescent's behaviour is peer group, social media and the role models. They start to dress up like them, copy their talking style, hair styles but at the end when they fail to do it or do not get any appreciation or attention they become depressed, by peer pressure or any other reason they become substance user. According to Lawrence and Patton, "one in four young people will have a mental disorder at any point of time, most commonly anxiety, depression and substance use disorders.

Identity Crisis:

Adolescents turn out very much conscious about themselves. At that time they formed personal and social identity. So always they try to be the central of attraction. They want attention from others. They explore different roles, behaviors, and ideologies at that time and as well as they think and want appreciation from others mainly from peer groups and then parent. Erik Erikson addressed this problem behaviour of adolescents in his psycho-social theory of personality as identity versus role confusion. So identity crisis also a great problem of adolescents. They are still trying to establish who they are and it end in more difficult and challenging for them. Sudden physical development and secretion of hormones lead their problem in a more complicated manner. They can't understand what should they will do. They try to avoid doing the things which are socially appropriate for them.

Adolescence- pregnancy:

Emotional development is also stormy, problematic and conflicting. Self identity and independence is very much prevailing in adolescents. They get influence from group peer group and show more sympathy and affection and attraction towards opposite sex and cause pre-mature pregnancy or adolescence- pregnancy. According to WHO, "In 2005, about 47 female per 1000 had children well under the age 20. In the developing world about 2.5 millions female under the age of 16 and 16 millions female of 15-19 year old have children each year."

Anorexia nervosa:

Adolescent girls mainly become more emotional at this stage, because of hormonal imbalance. They suddenly feel and behave like an adult. They are prone to mood swings and impulsivity is also there. Their emotions including male adolescents can be very much unpredictive. At the same time they do not like to treat as adult and also hate being taken as child or young. It hard to know what actually going on in their mind, what makes them happy or what depressed them or annoys them. They try to do only the things which she wants and focused more about ideal body. The pressure of keeping or making an ideal body self is mainly come from peer group and sometimes social media also. As at that time role model plays an important role for adolescent, so they want to become like them and these cause the illness anorexia nervosa (literally,"nervour lack of appetite") and also make them narcissist. Mainly in between 16 to 19 years old girls suffer by these behavioral problems.

According to Richards (1982)"the number of young people diagnosed as having anorexia has doubled in each decade over the last 30 years"

So it is very clear that the sense of ideal body self mainly in girls increasing day by day and the adolescents who have a distorted body image mainly they suffer by it. Dieting itself is not the main reason of anorexia but it can function as a trigger. Many adolescent girls first started their dieting to lose weight but after sometimes it can cause of this problem. When after losing some weight, they started to gain weight, it causes great distress and guilt in them.

Attention seeking behavior:

The reason behind the illness is short of self hurting activity and central theme of it is getting attention. They want to become the most beautiful one mainly in her peer group. They want their beauty to be noticed, appreciated and felt and as well as want importance and value from others. But most of the time when they feel they have not been noticed, appreciated or felt by others, they get hurt and become depressed and finally cause to do suicide which is one of the greatest behavioral problems in adolescents

Suicidal Tendency:

Many adolescents who try or attempt suicide they actually have a poor coping strategy and bad mental health condition. They face problem to cope up with the situations like stressful situation in school and family, rejection, breakups or any type of failure. Sometimes when they do not get attention or neglected by parents they take this step. They cannot find any solution and they think nothing has left, they cannot turn their lives around and they choose suicide as ultimate solution. "Suicide is the second leading cause of death, following motor vehicle accidents-among teenagers and young adults." "On average, adolescents aged 15 to 19 years have an annual suicide rate of about 1 in10000 people. Among youths 12-16 years of age up to 10% of boys and 20% of girls have considered suicide."

Stress and poor coping Skill:

As mentioned earlier, one leading cause of suicide and one prevailing behavioral problem of adolescents are stress and poor coping strategies. According to Lazarus and Folkman(1984),"psychological stress is a peculiar relationship between the individual and his environment, which the former judges menacing or beyond his recourses and potentially dangerous for his well being." In general, adolescence is the complicated as well as critical time in the development and adopting and practices the coping skills. When adolescents were child, they mostly use emotion-centered coping behaviour, but in adolescence they learn to control their emotions in a more culturally accepted way. So now they adopt purely cognitive coping skills or strategies

'Adolescents have often been described as a period with stress and tension.'(Blos,1979). So stress is the basic root problem of this stage. When situation is not going according to their wish, when they face failure, problem in interpersonal relationship, breakups or any other problems related to family and academic, they start to being anxious. They cannot find enough resources to cope with this stressful situation and become so much stressed that they cannot control their emotions and it is one of the reason to start another maladaptive behaviour. That is Substance use.

Substance use:

"During adolescence one is vulnerable to engaging in a lot of risky behaviors. Substance abuse is one such set of behaviors."

"According to the 2011 Youth Risk Behavior Surveillance Survey in United States, 44.7% of high school students had ever smoked cigarettes; 18.1% of students reported current cigarette use; 7.7% of students reported current smokeless tobacco use (e.g., chewing tobacco, snuff, or dip); 23.4% of students reported current tobacco use which included cigarette use, smokeless tobacco use, or cigar use; 70.8% of students had ever drunk alcohol; 38.7% reported current alcohol use; 21.9% of students engaged in binge drinking; 24.1% of students had ridden one or more times in a vehicle driven by someone who had been drinking alcohol; 8.2% of students had driven a vehicle one or more times when they had been drinking alcohol; 39.9% of students had ever used marijuana; 23.1% of students reported current marijuana use; 6.8% of students had ever used cocaine; 3% reported current cocaine use; 11.4% had ever used inhalants; 8.2% had ever used ecstasy; 2.9% of students had ever used heroin; and 3.8% of students had ever used methamphetamines" (Eaton et al., 2012)

Drugs, alcohol are products or substances that give people pleasure for some time and it changes the way people think or look their surroundings. This maladaptive behaviour patterns often lead to clinically significant problem. Many scientific studies have been done to know about the main reason of substance use in adolescents. But there is no primary reason which mainly identifies as the origin of consumption. There are some common factors that are identified worldwide culturally. Adolescent start to use substance to get acceptance from peer and self too, relaxation, for fun, to get pleasure or to taste a new things being curious, developing confidence, lack of family structure etc.

Sometimes stress causes by family conflicts or broken family play an important and significant role in adolescent's life to adopt this mal practices. These substances use leads to adopt a greater problem that is conduct disorder.

Conduct disorder:

Conduct disorder in adolescents can have onset before ten years but mainly it is seen in adolescents. It is one of the basic behavioral problems in adolescents that have a greater risk in future. It has recitative and persistent pattern of behavior. Adolescents try to violate the basic norms and rules of society, do not follow the rules in school and do not follow the instructions of parent and teachers. They face a great problem in Interpersonal relations, social and academic also. It is the disruptive and violent behaviour and adolescents have problems to follow the societal rules.

From a study," it is known that conduct disorder is mostly seen in boys than girls. The study also indicates "in general populations for boys it ranges from6%to 16% while the rate among girls range from 2% to 9%."

It is very common for adolescents that they have behavioral related problems in this developmental age. But this problem considers as conduct disorder when it lasts long, creates problems for family and hampered the peace of family and their behavior goes against societal norms and disrupts their mental health. Adolescents with this problem tend to show frequent temper-tantrums, mood-swings, easily show irritability and also have low self esteem.

Low socioeconomic status, problems with moral awareness, dysfunctional family life, substance abuse in family, Abuse in childhood, brain injuries etc lead this disorder. If conduct disorder continues beyond eighteen years, then it may cause the problem of antisocial personality disorder.

Conclusion:

"Adolescence is "the period of life that starts with the biological, hormonal and physical changes of puberty and ends at the age at which an individual attains a stable, independent role in society." (Balocchini, Chiamenti, & Lamborghini, 2013, p. 191). As adolescence stage itself is a crucial and complicated stage therefore adolescents need help to understand the inside-out changes and they need proper guidance. In prevention approaches after parent teacher educators also play an important role to guide these adolescents and help them to get better solution of their problems. The role of a teacher should be a friend, philosopher guide and a counselor who always be ready to listen them. Beside it adolescence education and different life skills should be imparted to adolescent's school curriculum to help them to transit as adult in a smooth and successful way. Different awareness and motivational program need to be arranged. Imparting the adolescence education is very much important for them to clear their doubts and myths, to provide encouragement and support and making them sensible towards the society as well as world and help them to be a productive member of the society.

CHAPTER EIGHTEEN

KEY TO KNOWLEDGE-KNOW TO UNKNOWNS

Introduction:

Knowledge is defined as justified true belief about something. From the ancient time the concept of knowledge has been very much concerned area in philosophy. In other language the history and nature of knowledge has been a central concern in philosophy. The theory of knowledge is a part of a branch of philosophy that is known as 'epistemology.' Sometimes this branch of philosophy is defined as the study of knowledge. Epistemology comes from 'espistemel' which is a Greek word, meaning ' knowledge' and 'logos' meaning ' discourse' or ' science'. Epistemology mainly concerned with three question or areas related to knowledge, that are- What is knowledge, how knowledge is acquired and what do people know and so on.

A universally accepted definition of knowledge is not possible to give anyone. Different scholars defined this term 'knowledge' according to their line of studies and interest domains.

Some scholars define Knowledge from recognize point of view. They said," the word Knowledge has its roots word.'recognization'. We know only those things that we recognize. So to bring the recognized experiences into the territory of Knowledge, people do some mental process like first they process their experiences and then share it to give different mental forms. So people can identify and store the experiences as their knowledge.

Definition:

The term knowledge is recorded at least by the 1300s as the Middle English *knouleche,* "This word combines the verb 'know' (a verb that means "to perceive or understand as fact or truth; to apprehend clearly and with certainty") and *'leche',* it also may be related to the same suffix wedlock and conveys a sense of "action, practice, or state.' Daniel Bell, the Harvard University Professor of Sociology while discussing 'knowledge' as the moving force of the Post-industrial Society, gives a comprehensive definition of knowledge as follows:

"Knowledge is an organized set of statement of fact or an idea, presenting a reasoned judgment or an experimental result, which is transmitted to others through some communication medium, is some systematic form. Knowledge consists of new judgments (Research and Scholarship) or presentation of older judgments as exemplified in text books, teaching and learning and collected as library and archival material."

Alvin Toffler, "the well known author of Future Shock, Third Wave and Power Shift, gives another meaning of knowledge, which includes data, information,images and imagery, as well as attitudes, values and other symbolic productsof society whether true, approximate or even false."

In the fast-emerging new discipline of 'Knowledge Management', Davenport defines "Knowledge is a fluid mix of framed experience, values, contextual information, and expert insight that provides an environment and framework for

evaluating and incorporating new experiences and information. It originates and is applied in the minds of knower. In organizations, it often becomes embedded not only in documents or repositories but also in organizational routines, processes, practices, and norms."

So knowledge basically a subjective experience including data, information, values etc which are mainly available in society by using some medium like books, journal, Social media etc.

Division of Knowledge-3

Knowledge has different divisions knowledge is obtained by some way or manner. So depending on this manner, knowledge can be divided into three following points-

A. A priori knowledge, B) A posteriori knowledge, C) Experienced knowledge.

A) Priori knowledge: Priori means 'before'. This type knowledge's truthfulness or falsify can be measured or decided before experience. In Philosophy, mainly in traditional philosophy, this type of knowledge is known as superior to all other knowledge. The analytical propositions are come under this type of knowledge.

In analytical propositions, the words in the sentences expressing the truth, logic of these sentences itself tell people that the sentence is true. So there is no need to variety, its truth or falsity with experience or anything, it decided by pure reason. Example of this proposition is, "All triangles have three sides."

B)A posteriori knowledge: This type of knowledge need different methods like observation and verification. So to gain posteriori knowledge about something verifications and experience is very much needed. Accurate observation and exact description is the major key point in the posteriori knowledge.

So, here under this the synthetic propositions come and the truth or falsity of these propositions can be decided or verified only by observation and verification. So its truth or falsity depends upon the facts about thre world. So scientific knowledge is one of the examples of this type knowledge.

C) Experienced knowledge: Maximum knowledge that people have about this world come from mainly experience. Experience is the basic theme in this type of knowledge. This type knowledge is always tentative and to get value it must be always experienced.

Types of Knowledge: Knowledge stands for the information and facts that people acquire through knowledge. Knowledge is also the familiarity people gained by experience and recognization of a fact or situation. There are so much confusion and disagreement over the different types of knowledge, so no such list of types is there. According to Krathwohl (2002) has categorized knowledge into four types-A) Factual Knowledge B) Conceptual knowledge, C) Procedural knowledge and D) Metacognitive knowledge.

A) Factual knowledge: This type knowledge is related to the knowledge of terminologies, facts, major ideas, specific details of a particular field or domain. This type of knowledge people store in their mind to use when they need in some certain situation. People gathered factual knowledge by exposure, repetition, and commitment to memory.

B) Conceptual Knowledge: This knowledge can be defined as knowing information about theories, models, classification, generalization and rules of a particular topic or domain.

C) Procedural Knowledge: This knowledge related to knowing subject-specific skills, techniques-methods, algorithms, method of inquiry and ability to select particular procedure for a topic. It transfers the knowledge from 'what' to 'how.'

D) Meta-Cognitive-Knowledge: This can be defined as a strategic knowledge that people use to solve problems and to do cognitive tasks. This is also understood as self knowledge. Human beings are complex .To know oneself and others complex and critical behaviors meta-cognitive knowledge is useful and helpful too.

Sources of Knowledge: There are many things which act as a source of knowledge. But the main sources are-

A) Through Sense Organs- People know more things about the external world, about surroundings and so on through our sense organs. Our sense organs are the primary source of getting knowledge about the characteristics of external world. This type of knowledge is also known as sensory knowledge. Explicit and implicit knowledge come under this of knowledge that mainly guides human being to understand the world through sense organs.

B) Reasoning: It is mainly two types- deductive reasoning and inductive reasoning. Mainly deductive type reasoning is the most familiar reasoning. It is also known as deduction. Deductive reasoning is a type which people can use in both academic field and everyday life. By this way they gain knowledge, mainly knowledge related to mathematics and computer programming can get from these deductive reasoning.

Inductive reasoning really helpful in everyday life to build the understanding and knowledge about the world. This reasoning is also known as inductive logic. Here general conclusions are drawn from as set of specific observation. So many eminent educationalist and research person has termed it as" bottom-up-logic"

So these two type reasoning very much helpful to get knowledge about the world and mainly help to get knowledge about academic purposes.

c) Authority: It is the secondary source of knowledge. People accept and keep it in mind because; they get this information from authority like teacher, parent sometimes senior peer groups also. So truth of this type knowledge is depends on the trust and faithful towards authority.

Here the authority related persons should have enough in depth knowledge in their field and they should be knowledgeable. They can pride relevant proof and explanation for the knowledge he is providing to others.

Nature of Knowledge:

i. Knowledge can be limited and unlimited. Person's knowledge about different domains is not same. Knowledge about a domain is unlimited means he has in depth knowledge about this domain but in the same person for another discipline may be ha has limited amount of knowledge.

v. Knowledge is always depending on verification and examination. Without this, truthfulness or falsity of knowledge cannot be tested.

v. Knowledge is always depending on information. Information is the basic source of knowledge.

v. Knowledge never corrosion. After getting Knowledge about something it never decay and it always be worthy for the person in every situation.

v. Knowledge is useful in every aspects of a human being for his daily life work. From doing a single take to solve difficult problems, knowledge meet all the requirements

v. Knowledge is abstract. The understanding of knowledge of a particular topic for different people is differ one from another and it happens only for the abstract nature of knowledge.

v. Knowledge has a social nature. It is available in equal proportions to each and everyone in a society but how much one will take it totally depends on the person only.

v. Knowledge can be acquired by experience. Human gather much amount of data from their life experience with interacting others and from other sources of knowledge.

v. Knowledge is cumulative. Human beings pass knowledge one generation to others. So it grows and develops and transmits one generation to the next.

v. Through Different specialized techniques knowledge is gained and transmitted.

Knowledge and Doing- Differentiation:

Knowledge is the part of the intellectual mind that is conscious mind. Knowledge is related to gain information, facts, rules, regulations, facts etc about a particular topic or about some different topic. To gain this V, people use different media like books, journals, articles, institutions etc. These are the main sources of Knowledge.

Doing is a part of emotional mind that is conscious and subconscious both. Sometimes what people do they don't know. If others ask them why you are doing so, they cannot give answer. It is a sort of or result of habits. These habits are developed over time. There is said that knowledge becomes useless, when nothing is done from thus knowledge.

So there is a key difference between these two- Knowledge and doing. Knowledge is basically a theoretical or practical understanding of a topic, subject or anything. Doing is performing an action. That has a consequence. But there is no consequence of knowing or getting Knowledge about something.

Knowledge is basically theoretical aspects where doing is related to practical aspect of something.

To Knowledge about a domain there is no influence of doing. Only understanding level is there. But in doing something there has influence of different factors and knowledge is one of them.

I know, but I don't do....,

Sometimes people do the just opposite of his knowledge only depending on his belief about the subject. Foe example, a person has depth knowledge about superstition and its bad impact but he does and practices many superstitious things because his belief and his family use to do such type of things.

So with this straight differentiation, there is a relation between these two. Before doing something if people have enough knowledge about the matter then it becomes easy to him to be aware about the consequences. It also helps to interpret the situation and according to it, people can do or perform.

Knowledge and thinking- Differentiation:

Knowledge as mainly related to theoretical based. "The word knowledge first defined as 'acquaintance with facts, truths or principle's a form of study or investigation." So knowledge is always lead to some factual, logical information that has a true sense in reality always. Knowledge is a fact but how this knowledge people can use in real situation in different aspects, it depends on a person's thinking skill. Thinking can be defined as the cpgnitive process that act as a mediator in between a stimuli that is situation and a response.

So thinking is a process to use the appropriate knowledge in a appropriate situation by first calculating the situational need. Knowledge is not a process. Knowledge is only gained by collecting in-depth information about something. And knowledge is always a fact that never changes depending on the person's thinking pattern. For example- some people may think the shape of the world is like an balloon, some may think the shape is oval but the fact is it is round which cannot change by any means and people can get this facts by knowledge from a source that is book. So knowledge is permanent.

Some educationists have given more importance on thinking than knowledge. As knowledge is more thepry based and thinking is more practical and reality oriented. They focus on thinking that it is more useful in a 'situation based on problem' To solve this situation thinking is more important. Because thinking include the problem solving skill. Step by step problem solving situation. Sometime a person have much knowledge about different things but in a problem solving situation lack of thinking skill, he cannot meet the situational need or does not do the needful.

Thinking is actually more depending on the assumed knowledge or sometimes thinking can be defined as a assumed knowledge. But knowledge itself is experiential based on observation and depends on verification.

More often, knowledge about something is not subjective bit its universal. When people get some fact about a subject, it is equal and same for people A to people Z. Means to everyone. Whereas thinking is subjective and individual differences is there. With having same amount of knowledge in a particular topic, one people's thinking pattern is totally different from another one.

Knowledge and feeling- Differentiation:
Knowledge is getting information by different available sources from our society. But feeling is totally a cognitive activity and part of human emotion. Knowledge is totally an abstract thing. Where feeling is an emotional state.

There is also a massive difference that is knowledge is related the left part of the brain where feeling is related with the right part of the brain.

These two can influence each other. People, when face a situation where they cant, find solution they can feel the lack of knowledge state. In other way when people get of information and gain knowledge about a particular thing then in between them feeling of satisfaction comes.

Conclusion:

Knowledge is basically a huge, complicated and complex context to different educationists. They are continuing to know the actual definition or meaning of knowledge. From all these above-mentioned context and facts about knowledge discovers different things related to knowledge. Knowledge is useful in every aspects of a human being for his daily life work. From doing a single take to solve difficult problems, knowledge meets all the requirements. Feeling, doing and think all has some differentiation with knowledge, beside it each one is interlinked with knowledge. So knowledge is a broader concept that never decades.

Bibliography

- Balocchini, E., Chiamenti, G., & Lamborghini, A. (2013). Adolescents: Which risks for their life and health? Journal of Preventive Medicine & Hygiene, 54(4), 191-194
- Bhutta Waqar Ahmad," (2009). "Social Work", Lahore: Advanced Publishers, pp-66-67.
- Bhutta Waqar Ahmad," (2009). "Social Work", Lahore: Advanced Publishers, pp-64-66.
- Davenport, Thomas H. and Prusak, K. Lawrence (1998). *Working Knowledge: How Organizations Manage What They Know.* Boston, MA: Harvard BusinessSchool Press.
- Eaton, D. K., Kann, L., Kinchen, S., Shanklin, S., Flint, K. H., Hawkins, J., ... Centers for Disease Control and Prevention (CDC). (2012). Youth risk behavior surveillance - United States, 2011. Morbidity and Mortality Weekly Report Surveillance Summaries, 61(4), 1-162.
- Editor, (1988) " A comprehensive report on Madaris' efficacy" Islamabad: Ministry of religious affairs, pp-8-9.
- Edward Kang (April 4, 2019)" Research backed studying techniques, derived from www.edutopia.org, derived on 15th July, 2021, p-1.
- Edward Kang (April 4, 2019)" Research backed studying techniques, derived from www.edutopia.org, derived on 15th July, 2021, pp-1-5.
- Emma Chiappetta (June 18, 2021) "Cultivating Number sense among middle &high school students", derived from www.edutopia.org, pp-1-5.
- Gupta, Pushkrit and Puja (2010). A Study on Moral Judgement Ability of Pre-adolescent Children of Public Schools. International Journal of Education and Allied Sciences.July-Dec. 2010, Volume 2, No. 2, pp. 73-86 ISSN-0975-8380, Online ISSN-2231-4733
- Gupta. K.M. (1988): Training-cum-Research Project in value orientation, value Analysis Model, New Delhi, NCERT, Dept. of Teacher Education.
- Hammond. M. and Emle, Z.(2007. Attitudes to institutional authority, trength of support for moral values and maturity of socio-moral

reasoning. Retrieved from www.researchgate.com

- Hurlock Elizabeth (1974): A Study of the correlates of value system of college students Experiments Vol. XXII (8)
- Jyothi Joshi and Leena Poornachand,J (1994): "Moral values among adolescents belonging to joint and nuclear families", Journal of Indian Education, vol.19, No:4-5, PP: 85-87.
- Kemp, D. A. (1976). *The Nature of Knowledge. An Introduction for Librarians*. London: Clive Bingley.
- Khalid saleem Mansoor (2003) "Deeni Madaris mey taleem", Islamabad: Institute of policy studies, pp-30-37.
- Knobloch H, Pasamanick B. Gesell and Amatruda's developmental diagnosis. New York: Harper & Row, 1974.
- Krathwohl, D. R. (2002). A revision of Bloom's taxonomy: An overview. *Theory into Practice, 41*(4), 212-218.
- Loeber, R., & Keenan, K. (1994). Interaction between conduct disorder and its comorbid behavioral pathways as mediators of outcome. Journal of Clinical Child conditions: Effects of age and gender. Clinical Psychology Review, 14(6), 497- Psychology, 30(4), 536-551. 523.
- Loeber, R., Wung, P., Keenan, K., Giroux, B., Stouthamer-Loeber, M., Van Kammen, W. Rubin, K. H., & Mills, R. S. (1991). Conceptualizing developmental pathways to B., & Maugham, B. (1993). Developmental pathways in disruptive child behavior. internalizing disorders in childhood. Canadian Journal of Behavioural Development and Psychopathology, 5(1-2), 103-133
- Lowery GH. Growth and development of children. Chicago: Year Book Medical Publishers, 1978.
- Mallaradhya.B.K. (1975): Study of Moral and Religious Instruction in the Higher Primary Schools in
- Mangal S.K. (2013) "Advanced Educational Psychology", 2nd Ed. Published by Ashoke k.Ghosh PHI Learning Pvt. Ltd Rimjhim House, ISBN: 978-81203-2038-3 Page No. : 112 - 117
- Mansoor Ali Akbar (1998) "Muslim Psychology", Lahore: Feroze Sons,pp-100-1-1.
- Masood Tahira Dr., (2017) "Why advice is ineffective", Lahore: Monthly periodical Turjuman-ul-quran, p-90.
- Monique Verhoeven, Astrid Mita poortuis & Monique Volman (March, 2019), " The role of schools in adolescents identity development, A literature Review, Educational Psychology Review Journal, Vol. 31,

issue1, pp-1-2.

- Mughal Tariq Mahmood, (2013) " Social Psychology', Lahore: Urdu Science Board, p-206.
- Mughal Tariq Mahmood,(2013) " Social Psychology', Lahore: Urdu Science Board, pp-218-221.
- Muhammad Amin Dr., (2004) "Islam aor Tazkiya Nafs", Lahore: Urdu Science Board, pp-607-608.
- Muhammad Asad Allama, (March 2009) " importance of Sunnah", Lahore: Turjuman-ul-Quran, pp-33-34.
- O'Brien,E., Asmar, R., Beilin, L., Imai, Y., Mallion,J. M., Mancia, G., &Parati, G.(2003). Definition, prevalence, and implications for assessment and treatment. Children and European Society of Hypertension recommendations for conventional, ambulatory Youth Services Review, 28(7), 761-779. and home blood pressure measurement. Journal of hypertension, 21(5),821-848.
- Rehman Khalid (2010) " Deeni Madaris, conditions, prospects and problems", Islamabad: Institute of policy studies, pp-17-19.
- Robyn Harper (August 2018), "Science of adolescent affect students learning : How body & brain development affect student learning," retrieved from www.allyed.org, Washington: Alliance for Excellent Education, p-1,
- Shahab Qudratullah (2004) "Shahab Nama", Lahore: Sang-e- Meel Publications, pp-230- 240.
- Shari Gent, (March 22, 2021) "12 strategies to inspire listening learning and self-control", derived from www. additudemag.com, derived on 16[Th] July, 2021,p-1.
- Shari Gent, (March 22, 2021) "12 strategies to inspire listening, learning and self-control", derived from www. additudemag.com, derived on 16[Th] July, 2021,pp-2-16.
- Taj Hassen and KH. Prabhu(2013) "Relationship between Moral judgement and Emotional competence of secondary school students." Journal of Educational & Psychology Research (vol- -3 vol-1) Jan 2013 ISSN 2230-9586 Page No : 20
- Tanner JM, Whitehouse RH, Takaishi M. Standardsfrom birth to maturity for height, weight, height velocity, and weight velocity: British children, 1965. Arch Dis Children. 1966;41:613.
- Tanner JM. Growth at adolescence. 2nd end. Oxford: Blackwell, 1962.
- Tripathi,D.K & Misra.G (1979) : Development of moral judgement in

Indian children Psuchologia : An International journal of psychology in the Orient, 22, 164-169.

- Walia, J.S (2011) "Development of Learner and Teaching Learning Process" – Published by Ahim Paul publishers, N.N. Gopal Naga Jalandhar city (Punjab) Printed at – Bright Printers,Jalandhar, Page No : 138-42

- Wetzel NC. In: Glasser O, Ed. Medical physics. Chicago: Year Book Medical Publishers, 1944.

- World Health Organization. 23 February 2018. Retrieved 2 November 2018

- https://www.economicsdiscussion.net/management/personality/personality-introduction/32465

- https://www.verywellmind.com/who-were-the-neo-freudians-2795576

- https://courses.lumenlearning.com/boundless-psychology/chapter/trait-perspectives-on-personality/

- https://www.coursehero.com/file/p4t8mfk/Conclusion-The-study-of-the-theories-of-personality-is-important-for-students/#:~:text=described%20my%20personality.-,Conclusion%20The%20study%20of%20the%20t

- https://www.britannica.com/topic/personality

- https://www.verywellmind.com/what-is-personality-2795416

- https://courses.lumenlearning.com/boundless-psychology/chapter/introduction-to-personality/

- https://www.apa.org/topics/personalityhttps://medbroadcast.com/condition/getcondition/adolescent-suicide

- https://physicscatalyst.com/graduation/knowledge-meaning-types-sources/

- https://learningstrategist.org/2018/03/01/4-types-of-knowledge/

- http://absolutetruth.squarespace.com/blog/2018/1/3/feeling-vs-knowing